ON THE TIP OF MY TONGUE

ON THE TIP OF MY TONGUE

THE PERFECT WORD FOR EVERY LIFE MOMENT

TOM READ WILSON

Aurum

First published in 2022 by Aurum
an imprint of the Quarto Group
1 Triptych Place
London SE1 9SH, United Kingdom

www.Quarto.com/Aurum

A catalogue record for this book is
available from the British Library.

ISBN: 978-0-7112-7667-3
Ebook ISBN: 978-0-7112-7669-7
Audiobook ISBN: 978-0-7112-8130-1

3 4 5 6 7 8 9 10

Cover design by Emma Ewbank
Cover author photograph © Harry Cumming
Introduction page photograph © Nicky Johnston
Typeset in Gotham, Tungsten & Adobe Garamond Pro
Design concept by Josse Pickard
Designed by Isabel Eeles

Printed and bound by CPI Group (UK) Ltd,
Croydon, CR04YY

•••●

For my beloved family and friends,
who eternally delight me with their divergent tongues.

●•••

Contents

How to...

How to...

Introduction

Words are personal. As personal as it gets. We are as defined by words we refuse to use as by our favourites. Some words date and some are timeless. Some words wear their etymology like a glistening pendant and others hide it, pretending they have no relationship with it whatsoever. Words, I put it to you, are at least a thousand times more personal than the garments we wear or the pictures we hang.

We amass our collections of words and phrases throughout our lives. You may be a spry sapling of 30 who decides to 'spend a penny' rather than go to the loo because of your fondness for your maternal grandmother who uses the idiom often. You may love JOMO (joy of missing out) because it is less ubiquitous than FOMO (fear of missing out). You may have been 'triple jagged' because you live north of the Scottish border, whereas I have merely been jabbed. You may be flirting with giving 'leather-lunged-spouter' a renaissance when describing Adele, having heard Tallulah Bankhead say it about singers of her day and feeling – more than anything we currently say – it is *la phrase juste*. You may borrow from other languages when they put it more succinctly, or perhaps just to be a touch outré. You may have a special relationship with words like *queer, woke, lib, revisionism* because of your life, identity and history.

In short, our lexical cherry-picking depends on *everything* that makes us unique. My dearest chums and close family tell me that the question they are most frequently asked about me is, 'Does he talk like that all the time?' to which the answer is a sincere 'yes'. Mistaken on the radio for Fenella Fielding, Honor Blackman and Angela Lansbury,

I have a penchant for a polysyllable, inherited from my father, a former English teacher who also delights in language. After a recent lunch, he said 'This has been lovely but all-too-brief ...' then, as often happens, he was arrested by the dance of the synonyms '... fleeting, short-lived, ephemeral'. You can see how my condition started. It is incurable, as my father will attest. My mother is an impish, irreverent spirit. She is almost allergic to earnestness. If she can, she will stick a pin in anything approaching it. If someone, in awe or surprise, says, 'Well, well, well!' she is apt to respond, quick as a flash, 'Three holes in the ground!'

The best, most intimate portrait of our character is on the tip of our tongue. Within these pages lie some of my favourite examples. Some are my own, some are legendary, some are obscure and some I thought it egregious not to exhume. So, at this juncture, I invite you to tear open my etymological chocolate box, forget etiquette and simply guzzle.

Bon appétit!

VERBIVORE

vuhb·ih·vaw *noun*

Someone who enjoys
words and wordplay.

How to tool up before we get started

'Fret not nor fear', as my dad would say, these pages are not ferociously technical. In fact, I could not cope if they were. They are, foremost, designed to divert and tickle. I always aim to tickle. However, for ease of use, I have included some phonetic (fuh·neh·tuhk) pronunciations and grammatical parts of speech – noun, adjective or verb. You may also need the following words in your arsenal, as I am sure they will appear and I will have forgotten to define them, or it might spoil the flow if I did. Let us start with ...

Acronym

a·kruh·nim noun

Acronyms take the first letter of each word and assemble an independent word that represents the whole phrase. Time saving and catchy. My grandmother's FUFTB springs to mind (Full Up and Fit to Bust, *see* page 154) although for every FUFTB, I have 301 GOOMMS (Go On One More Morsel).

Aphorism

a·fuh·ri·zm noun

You could call this a truism, but an aphorism is ever so slightly more than that. It is a truism most beautifully wrapped. It comes from the Greek *aphorismos*, 'a pithy, punchy definition'. An aphorism is always succinct and, in its lyricism, seems to crystalise ideas. *The early bird catches the worm* is a popular example. For my favourite from these pages, we must thank the endlessly quotable Mary Poppins for *Enough is as good as a feast* (*see* page 64).

Coining

koy·nuhng verb

Coin is an Old French word meaning 'wedge'. Money could be made by inking the wedge and stamping the money with a permanent mark. You could leave your mark on language in the same way, by creating a word and inking it into the history books. Shakespeare did it all the time and we owe oodles of words to him. More on the Bard in short order (*see* pages 32–33).

Compound noun

kuhm·pownd nown noun

Compound nouns are common because it is human nature, when

new things, roles or places are created, to describe them using existing things, roles or places. So, a lighthouse is like a house but with a giant, swiveling light in it. A spaceship is a ship that can sail through space. Sometimes they are hyphenated, sometimes each stands alone while gaily flanking each other, like my favourite, appearing shortly, powder room (*see* page 77).

Contraction

kuhn • trak • shn noun

When a muscle contracts, it shortens, but still contains the same amount of tissue. This can happen with words, too. My Liverpudlian brother-in-law might offer me a *bevvy* when I visit. This is a very attractive contraction of *beverage*, meaning 'drink'. Although he has truncated the word, it has retained its full meaning.

Eponym

ep • uh • nim noun

An eponym is a word that comes from a person's name. A contraption might bear the name of its inventor, a profession the name of one of the first successes in the field, as we will discover with *thespian* (*see* page 21). A flower may even be an eponym, if the curls of its petals resemble the curls of its namesake's hair, as we will discover with *hyacinth* (*see* page 36).

Etymology

eh • tuh • mo • luh • jee noun

Not to be confused with entomology, the study of bugs, etymology is the study of the origins of words. An etymologist takes the complete jigsaw that every word offers and breaks it into pieces to see what each constituent part contributes to the whole.

Homophone

ho • muh • fown noun

Homophones are simpler than they sound and are all to do with sound as opposed to (often) appearance. From the Greek *homos*, meaning 'same' and *phone*, meaning 'sound', the same roots found in *homosexual*, romantically drawn to the 'same sex', and *telephone*, a device for hearing 'far-off sounds'. Homophones *sound* the same but may not share the same spelling or provenance. *Knights* and *nights* to the ear are identical but to the eye are not. *Bats* with wings and *bats* for cricket are identical to eye *and* ear, so these homophones are dependent on context, whether scribbled or uttered.

Idiom

i • dee • uhm noun

Idioms are collections of words where the words themselves lose their respective identities to serve the meaning of the whole. An idiom that immediately springs to mind from these pages is *green gowning* (*see* page 131). It has nothing directly to do with greenness or grass, but instead is a nod to the activity denoted by green grass stains on the garments of lovers emerging from a field.

Lexical

lek • suh • kl adjective

Lexicon comes from the Greek *legein*, meaning 'speak'. Our lexicons are, in fact, the *words* we speak. You could call this whole book a lexical web, connecting and gluing together the stories of words.

Onomatopoeia

o • nuh • ma • tuh • pee • uh *noun*

Onomatopoeic words are such fun to say because they are words that have been invented as soundalikes. *Squelch* sounds like the noise created by stepping in a cowpat, *burp* sounds like that bugle ring that comes out of you when you ingest something fizzy too fast, and *plop* sounds like a pebble as it makes contact with a pond and disappears from view.

Portmanteau

pawt • man • tow *noun*

We have Lewis Carroll, author of *Alice's Adventures in Wonderland* and *Alice Through the Looking Glass* to thank for this one. You may remember the scene in the book where Alice meets Humpty Dumpty and asks the rather irascible egg to dissect the poem 'Jabberwocky'. Much of Humpty's elucidation comes from decoding the fused-together words. He explains that *chortle* is a combination of 'chuckle' and 'snort' and *slithy* is a combination of 'slimy' and 'lithe'. In Carroll's day, writers would keep their manuscripts in order by carrying them in a portmanteau, a smart carry case of two constituent parts, linked by an elegant clasp in the centre. It occurred to Carroll that his cleaving and re-stitching of words in 'Jabberwocky' was the lexical version of this case, so 'portmanteau' gained a second definition, one pertaining to words.

Skeuomorph

skyoo • uh • morf *noun*

Here is another portmanteau! From *skeuos*, 'container' and *morphē*, 'shape', it is something that contains, conjures or imitates the shape and aesthetic of a different thing but not, necessarily, that thing's behaviour. The linguistic variety usually happens

PALCHRONY

pal•kruh•nee *noun*

My own portmanteau for
being in wonderful synchrony
with a chum.

when time and technology have marched on, leaving language behind. Take *hanging up* the phone. No one has a telephone where you hang the receiver anymore (if you can't conjure this image, think Mr Banks in *Mary Poppins* after telephoning the police) and yet, when we press that little red circle on our smartphone to end a call, we still claim to be doing it. We are, linguistically at least, imitating a lost action. In fact, even the image within the red circle nods, skeuomorphically, to the obsolete act.

How to...
speak like
a thespian

I am an erstwhile thespian. Thespians are, naturally, instinctive logophiles. Part of the joy of the theatre is masticating on challenging polysyllables produced by minds that hover in astral planes above us, cerebrally speaking. In addition to the words found in wonderful plays and musicals authored for the stage, there is the lexicon of the community that orbits the stage: directors, actors, stagehands, et al. The first of these was Thespis ...

Thespian

theh•spee•uhn *adjective noun*

The word *thespian* belongs to one of my favourite word groups: the eponym. This is when a word comes from a person's name. There are oodles! *Bloomers* from American post-mistress and feminist, Amelia Bloomer, *cardigan* from the 7th Earl of Cardigan, *zephyr* because of the Greek god of the wind, and on and on. Thespis is often called the father of Greek Tragedy. Legend has it that he was the first poet ever to recite on a public stage. No wonder his name blesses all who have subsequently scuffed the boards.

Theatre

thee•uh•tuh *noun*

This word, which has such import in my life, comes from the Greek, where the theatre's story began. *Theasthai* is the Greek stem meaning 'to behold'. *Theatron* was, in turn, the place of *united beholding* for Greek audiences. These were, of course, open-air sites of beholding, but 'houses of beholding' were to follow and these, I think, are my personal favourites. When thespians become movie stars, they may also become matinee idols ...

Matinee

ma•tuh•nay *noun*

Matutinus is from Latin and means 'pertaining to morning'. The early bird might engage in many *matinal* or 'morning' activities or, for the even more highfalutin, matutinal activities. Why then, should a matinee, famously an afternoon performance, be linked to our root? Because these performances were originally, and most horrifyingly for the thespians reading (and writing) these pages, in the morning! French thespians would play to packed houses in these morning performances. Gradually, however, the notion of two show days and the convenience of the smaller hiatus, allowing actors brief surcease to dine between afternoon and evening shows without travel, seemed to suit management and companies better. Nevertheless, in theatrical circles, these days are still known as the *dreaded doubles*. Actors would be lost without ...

Consonants
kon•suh•nuhnts adjective noun

Sonor is the Latin root meaning 'sound'. So *sonic* is not merely an adorable little blue hedgehog, but 'pertaining to sound'. It follows, then, that *sonorous* should mean 'great sound' that generously pervades the air. But *consonant*? The vowels here are key, because, etymologically, consonant means 'sounding with' and, of course, consonants only can be sounded properly if preceded or followed by a vowel. In our sonorous world these alphabet chums are truly co-dependent!

Corpsing
kawps•ing verb

One of the legendary perils of the theatre. This is an act of homicide by the actor. It is killing one's own character. Turning it into a corpse. Dictionary definitions of corpsing always describe the three main ways an actor can murder their creation. The list includes, but is not limited to, dropping your character's accent, forgetting your lines or laughing in unintended places. However, IRL corpsing is only ever used to describe the latter. I am a very good corpser (or very bad, depending on your POV). The condition is woefully exacerbated when two corpsers meet. There was one pantomime in particular, *Sleeping Beauty* where I met my match. I was playing the evil fairy Maleficent, renamed

Firena. Typically, our matinees contained local school children in the front three rows of the stalls. One day, Row A had a cherubic boy of six. I had a scene with my fellow corpser, the prince, where I delineated part of my heinous plan. As I wrapped up my wicked plot, the cherub stood and shouted, 'Fuck off and die.' I defy milder corpsers than we to continue giggle-free after that.

Shake the ladder

Ginger Rogers is one of the many actors who talks about this wonderful Broadway idiom of yesteryear. If you have ever explored the wings of a theatre, you will know that you invariably find a ladder or seven. Often, parts will require that an actor enters the stage in a flurry of excitement, rage or joy. How does one go from zero to 100 while quietly awaiting one's entrance in the wings? One answer is a vigorous shake of the ladder in the wings. It might just get you hot under the collar, red-faced and energised in time for your entrance to wow spectators with your authenticity!

The Green Room

There are a handful of explanations as to the appellation of this most deliciously fabled quadrant of the theatre. My favourite is the theory that it comes from the cockney rhyming slang for 'stage': *greengage*. Beloved thespian friends of mine are still inclined to say, 'see you on the green', including my lovely chum, Harriet Thorpe, who will always round it off with the addendum, 'dear'. I suppose, therefore, it stands to reason that a communal room for actors that flanks the greengage (or green for short) should be called the Green Room. Here is another person you might see strutting their stuff with their hand up a bottom on the green ...

The ventriloquist

thuh • ven • tri • luh • kwuhst   noun

Venter is the Latin root meaning 'belly'. The ventricles of your heart are 'small bellies' because they are stomach-like cavities. How, then, does a performer who talks without moving their lips pertain to our gut-root? Because, like a human bagpipe the ventriloquist speaks directly from the belly, creating 'belly talk' and reducing dependence on those oh-so-visible lips! Who knew that this art was such a close relative of the good old-fashioned burp? Ventriloquism was considered so magical that there is an etymological nod to sorcery here, too, in the notion that the puppet's voice might belong to a belly-housed spectre.

Tenor

teh • nuh   noun

The tenor is custodian of many of the greatest numbers of theatre history. The voice part's appellation is due to tenor roles being characterised by stretchy, sustained musical phrases. The Latin root *ten* pops up everywhere, conveying different kinds of 'stretch'. *Tenuous* describes something slight or insubstantial as though stretched thin, and *tender* denotes the vulnerability of the overstretched, liable to tear. The *tenor*, by contrast, embodies a glorious stretch: stretching his larynx over long, rousing musical passages.

Eleven o'clock number

Here is a phrase I use metaphorically all the time. I use it to denote a climax. In lavish Broadway musicals, Act II was always structured in such a way that the protagonist's epiphanic moment would come via a stonking great song at the shank of the show. Think 'Rose's Turn' in *Gypsy* or 'A Boy Like That,

I Have a Love' in *West Side Story*. When the shows first opened on Broadway, these numbers would land at approximately eleven o'clock and would ...

Bring the house down

The *house* is a synonym for the theatre itself. Bringing it down sounds like something you might wish to avoid at all costs but, in fact, it is the performer's goal. It is based on the notion that the laughter is so uproarious, the clapping so thunderous, the cheers so vociferous that they threaten the very brickwork. The whole theatre is atremble with the delight of the crowd.

Dance and sing

These words are included in my descriptions of almost all my corporeal reactions. A superlative meal will make my *tastebuds dance*, a crossword will make my *grey cells dance*. Great melodies and wonderful voices *dance on my tympanic membrane*. Inspiring literature makes my *retinas sing*, as does art. A dynamic workout is apt to make my *bloodcells dance* and my *muscles sing*. It seems to me there is a loose rule as to whether my bits and bobs are singers or dancers. If there are oodles of them – bloodcells, tastebuds and the like – they will dance because there are enough of them to comprise a corps de ballet. If there are fewer, or just one of my bits – muscles, retinas, olfactory nerve – then singing somehow seems more apropos.

How to...
decline politely,
or impolitely

I am what is known, I think, as an extroverted introvert.
I adore doing a little turn at a party but do not really want
the party to orbit me. I love scintillating conversation but
often experience – contrary to the 'slow diminuendo'
that my friends describe – an instant bloom-off-my-rose
(*see* page 29) sensation and I know it is all over. In short,
I like to vacillate between extreme socialisation and cosy
solitude. If you are like me, it pays to have some *outs* in
your arsenal just in case ...

I'm too fucking busy, and vice versa.

– Dorothy Parker

My favourite *out* comes from the endlessly quotable Dorothy Parker. This was a telegram sent to her publisher from her honeymoon. The legendary poet and lover could legitimately say this either way round. I could not. Nevertheless, I include it as the neatest, scrummiest, bravest *out* there is.

My children are all very shy: they don't like to attend parties unless they know they're going to be the bride or the corpse.

**– Thomas Hepburn,
Katharine Hepburn's father**

Dorothy Parker was banned from Katharine Hepburn's opening nights forever after she damned the latter's performance in the Broadway play *The Lake*, by writing, 'Miss Hepburn ran the whole gamut of emotions – from A to B!' It cannot have helped Kate's vomit-inducing stage fright. Another place she experienced intense fear was at parties. Hepburn, to date, holds the record for most best actor wins at the Oscars (deliberately going gender neutral here since she tops the list in both sexes). However, she never attended the ceremony (other than to present an honorary Oscar). The reason for her absences ranks among her most highly tallied interview questions. She always neatly attributed it to shyness, citing her father's observation.

    This next excuse is one of my own. There are, naturally, occasions – though they are of course rare – where one is just too tired to attend a party. Tired, fatigued, flat: they all sound so beige and drear-full that I always find myself leaning toward euphemism instead. My favourite is *threadbare*. However, sometimes even *threadbare* gets a bit threadbare, so instead I reference the most celebrated of all threadbare pieces when I excuse myself, saying, 'I'm sorry but ... I have become the Bayeux Tapestry.'

The bloom is off my rose

Blimey! This is as useful a euphemism as I know. And I trot it out 'on the reg', as the kids say. I am at a curious juncture in my professional life where there are lots of early rises (filming tends to begin at sparrow's fart) coupled with occasional evening events (I am only seduced by those of a theatrical bent). If I do go to the latter with former looming the following day, the above perfectly describes my condition. You see, I have no diminuendo. Most of my contemporaries have a slow fade. I have a switch. I operate at the same velocity all evening, then suddenly stop functioning. That is my Cinderella time. I used to find conveying all of this difficult. These days I simply say, alas, *the bloom is off my rose*.

How to...
throw shade
(and keep your
dignity intact)

I don't know about you, but I am hopeless when it comes to insults. That is, I am hopeless at insults in the heat of the moment. Shortly after the altercation I think of the perfect comeback. Maddeningly, it has a habit of coming to you once you have slammed the door of your opponent's flat and are pounding the stairs to the foyer like a red-faced reverse-mountaineer in crampons. At this moment, you are consumed by ...

L'esprit de l'escalier

leh • spree deh • leh • scal • lee • ay noun

This untranslatable French expression literally means 'staircase wit'. It is the perfect description of the above condition of thinking of a divinely bruising rejoinder 'sur les escaliers'. Utterly infuriating! But it is such a common sensation that it deserves an expression all its own. Or even two ...

Treppenwitz

treh • pen • vits noun

German also gives us a 'staircase wit'. It describes the same infuriating feeling of a missed riposte. It seems that altitude exacerbates the argumentative spirit. Does anybody have a spat on the ground floor?

Insult

in • sult noun verb

We are about to get a little bit rude. Nevertheless, we shall retain our sense of play for, etymologically speaking, the word *insult* does. In Latin, the *in* part is 'on' and *saltare* 'to jump'. Insulting someone, therefore, is a verbal pounce that conjures an almost feline attack. I suppose, too, that insults are more inclined to spring from one, as opposed to compliments, which seep or ooze.

My insults, when they come – if they come – tend to be rather highfalutin. I like them to get vexingly lost in translation. As a result, I tend to avoid expletives and sarcasm. Incidentally, the etymology of both those words may well put you off, too.

Expletive

ex • plee • tiv adjective noun

Plenus is the Latin root meaning 'to fill'. Language is full of this root, and 'full' is precisely what *plenus*'s close relative *replete* means. *Deplete*, conversely, means to 'un-fill' or reduce. Now, where the fuck-pissing-tit-bollocks does swearing come into this? As I clunkily demonstrated in the previous sentence, an expletive is a *'filler* word'. Initially, *expletive* did not expressly refer to in-built naughtiness in a word but, etymologically, the word *expletive* seemed to imply these threads were mere 'fillers' in the rich tapestry of lexica that ought not to be mistaken for 'proper' speech. Well bollocks to that!

Sarcasm

saa • kaz • uhm noun

Sark is the Greek root meaning 'flesh'. It appears in *sarcoma*, which is a 'flesh-like' malignant tumour. *Sarcasm* is far more metaphorical. It is a 'ripping of flesh' with words so cutting that they are machete-like. Sarcasm really ought to come with the warning: next time you play with 'the lowest form of wit', remember its razor-like etymology! If, like me, you wish to get zestier and a little lyrical with your barbs, you could do a lot worse than old Billy Shakespeare ...

February face

The *February face* is, to me, the king of insults. I do not know whether it is the bounce of alliteration or the fact that the poetic veneer conceals the ultimate shade, but it is perfect.

'Why, what's the matter,
That you have such a February face,
So full of frost, of storm and cloudiness?'
– William Shakespeare, *Much Ado about Nothing*

Sticking to the face – that's an unfortunate phrase – but you know what I mean ...

'Thine face is not worth sunburning.'
                                    – William Shakespeare, *Henry V*

You cannot top Shakespeare when it comes to insulting a gloomy countenance, but it's hard to outsmart Oscar Wilde when insulting misguided sartorial efforts ...

'She was a curious woman, whose dresses always looked as if they'd been designed in a rage and put on in a tempest.'
                          – Oscar Wilde, *The Picture of Dorian Gray*

Or, from the very same,

'... she reminded one of a badly bound hymn-book'.

I suppose that the short delay caused by decoding these slights, especially when fired at you, makes you momentarily miss their sting. You are, in effect, too busy translating!

One of my favourite examples of this was when Julie Andrews was the only member of the Broadway company of *Victor/Victoria* to be nominated for the coveted Tony Award, the highest accolade in American Theatre. She called an impromptu press conference at the curtain call and said, in effect, that this was not a one-woman-show and that her company was like a family. Her sting came in the remark, 'I ... prefer to stand instead with the egregiously overlooked.'

She was saying, 'Sod your nomination, you've outrageously snubbed all my mates.' But the velvet glove of eloquence meant that New York's press, instead of gasping, were frantically looking up the word 'egregious'.

Egregious

uh•gree•juhs adjective
Greg is the Latin root meaning 'flock'. Perhaps Greggs bakery is not an appellation for a wizard entrepreneur patissier named

Gregory, but a crafty nod to the flocks that its vegan sausage rolls draw? *Greg*, the root – as opposed to Tom, Dick or Greg – flows neatly and logically into *congregate*: to 'flock together' and *gregarious*, liking the flock, i.e. sociable. But what about its rogue sibling *egregious*, meaning outrageous and notable? Egregious is cleaved from its etymological sisters because it means 'out of' or 'away from' the flock. After all, isn't it egregious that anyone should run away from Greggs?

Here are a few tough-to-translate barbs of my own:

Your countenance has all the joy of an apocalypse.

You're more Ursula and her ball than Pollyanna
and her prisms.

I'd sooner drink a pint of liquid lard
(than acquiesce to your request).

Most faces induce joy the moment the door opens:
somehow yours is in reverse.

How to ...
say it with
flowers

'People from a planet without flowers would think we must be mad with joy the whole time to have such things about us' wrote Iris Murdoch in *A Fairly Honourable Defeat*. I think she is right; any non-myopic Martian would surely be giddy with delight to behold such beauty. The Martian's light-headedness would surely only increase when they learn the etymology of some of our favourite blooms. I have arranged my favourites as a sort of lexical nosegay here:

Gladioli

gla • dee • ow • lai noun

Before we cut through floral etymology, let us spare a moment for the *gladiolus*. Who'd have thought that this tall, pretty bloom would be so close a relative of the mighty *gladiator*? *Gladius* is the Greek for 'sword' and while *gladiators* were sword-wielders, *gladioli* were the blooms identified by the 'little swords' at their base. Indeed, look at the leaves and you will see that they encircle the bloom like green daggers inserted handle-first into the earth.

Hyacinth

hai • uh • snth noun

Hyacinthus was such a beautiful young man that not one but two Greek Gods fell in love with him: Zephyr, the God of the West Wind, for whom Hyancinthus felt affection, and Apollo, whom Hyacinthus adored. Apollo and Hyancinthus enjoyed an exquisite love affair which, alas, met an untimely end thanks to jealous Zephyr. One day, Gods and mortals alike were playing games, and Apollo threw a discus. Zephyr blew his West Wind and threw the discus off course, hitting Hyacinthus in the head and killing him. Apollo's heart was broken. He begged Hades, fallen God of the Underworld, not to take Hyacincthus' soul but to conjure a new bloom from the blood he had shed from the injury. Hades acquiesced and the first hyacinth grew, with petals that arched like the curl of Hyacinthus's hair. The romantic nature of the flower has lived on, particularly for queer people. Oscar Wilde, a huge fan of Greek mythology, was incarcerated because of his homosexuality in 1895. From his prison cell he wrote an extended love letter entitled *De Profundis* to his 'hyacinth', the young, beautiful, ineffably selfish Lord Alfred Douglas (Bosie). Bestow these flowers on romantics, especially queer romantics.

Green carnation

green kaa • nay • shn *noun*

We cannot mention Oscar Wilde and flowers without mentioning the green carnation. The cryptic legend of this flower and its link with queer life is as complex as the whorl of its bloom. On the opening night of *Lady Windermere's Fan* in London in 1892, a mere three years before Wilde's incarceration, Wilde asked one of his actors to wear a green carnation in his buttonhole. Lo, the audience that night was dotted with the flowers in the buttonholes of Oscar's closest male friends. Given the extreme prejudice of the time in which he lived, Wilde could never openly unlock the code, but he came close, claiming they were only available at Goodyear's – a celebrated London florist – 'they grow them there'. The suggestion was that they do not belong to nature, their beauty is unnatural to the eyes of the society in which Wilde lived, but the beauty itself was unquestionable.

Carnation

kaa • nay • shn *noun*

There are two schools of thought concerning the carnation's name. One is that it is a minor mangling of coronation because of the crown-like points of its petals. This comes from the Latin *corona*, meaning 'crown', which is also present in *corona virus* because, under a microscope, the virus resembles a crown. My preferred theory is a bloodier theory. Carnation might come from the Latin *carnis* meaning 'flesh' which gives us the fleshy words like *carnal*, 'of the flesh' and *carnivore*, 'flesh eating'. This root gives us the colour *incarnadine*, which is the crimson of blood. In macabre literature you may have heard of people withdrawing incarnadine daggers, covered in gore. Incarnadine carnations are common, and I think this connection is highly probable. Perhaps this is why the flower gets such a bad rap and is even regarded as a symbol of death.

Peony

pee • uh • nee *noun*

Even Greek gods need a doctor. The physician who tended to them was Paiōn, whose name means 'healing' in Greek. Early Greek physicians believed that peony roots were diuretic, sedative and analgesic – almost a panacea. Stress relief and reduction of inflammation were also attributed to this wonder root. It is no surprise that early physicians felt this super tonic should take the name of the physician of the Gods! Cognisant of the historic reverence for this panacea, I take a peony tincture every day. Perhaps give peonies to those you want to see bounce back from an ailment, and in the same vein …

Pansy

pan • zee *noun*

We often send flowers to convey that somebody is in our thoughts. Curiously, we seldom send pansies to express this sentiment. Arguably, however, they are the most appropriate flower to send. It is built into the flower's name, from the French *pensée*, 'thought'. It was christened for exactly that reason. In mid-fifteenth-century France, these colourful cousins of the violet would be presented to demonstrate you were thinking of their recipient or planted in remembrance of somebody who had died.

Orchid

aw • kuhd *noun*

Send orchids to anyone but an *orchitis* sufferer: *Orchis* is the Greek root meaning 'testicle'. With a little augmentation we arrive at *orchitis*, which is a rather uncomfortable 'testicular inflammation'. How, then, do we then jump to botany with *orchid*? Quite a leap from balls, surely? If we travel south of the bloom to the bulb, we will be nearer the distinctive shape that inspired the name. However, when you consider just how many bulb-born sproutings we have in our gardens, I have to say, I think this name is a load of old bollocks.

Lupin

loo • pn noun

Perhaps the best flower to convey to the gardener whose weeds are rampant. These beautiful, purple, wand-like flowers take their name from the Latin *lupus*, meaning 'wolf'. *Lupus*, the disease, that results in ulceration shares this root. The connection probably lies in the behaviour of both flower and illness. *Lupins*, in Portugal, were very successful at chewing up weeds by occupying their space like a wolf-like predator. Lupus leaves flesh wounds as it attacks the skin in a wolf-like fashion. Even flowers are not safe from macabre etymology!

Geranium

juh • ray • nee • uhm noun

Flowers are seldom named for their bloom. Their names can be attributed to the soul they used to inhabit, the physician their powers imitate, the reason they are planted, their bulb or their impact on the soil. Here is a bloom that can be seen in almost every city window box but, again, owes its name to another part of its anatomy: its seedpod. The geranium seedpod looks just like the bill of a crane and, you guessed it, *geranos* is the Greek root meaning 'crane'. It also makes a perfect gift for die-hard Alan Jay Lerner fans (the lyricist responsible for *My Fair Lady* and *Gigi*) who authored my favourite internal rhyme in the song, 'Hurry! It's Lovely Up Here' from *On a Clear Day You Can See Forever* (1965) where he pairs 'geranium' with 'sub-terr-an-e–um'. Bliss!

Chrysanthemum

kruh•san•thuh•muhm *noun*

Perhaps the most perfect flower to give to any Anthea that you know, since it contains her name. This is no etymological accident. The name *Anthea* means flower, and the *anth* part of *chrysanthemum* is also delineating its floral identity. The prefix comes from the Greek *khrysos* meaning 'gold'. The prefix seems malapropos, as these fluffly flowers are riotous in colour, but the golden variety was certainly the most common and, I'm afraid, the lilac and blue varieties are purely a result of genetic tinkering.

Tulip

choo•luhp *noun*

A tulip is a turban. Etymologically speaking, that is. The Turkish word *tülbent* means 'turban' and it does not take much musing to see the link. Turbans are beautifully wrapped voile. The voile is fine enough to overlap without creating excessive bulk and the result is an attractive shape with visible leaves of voile. The tulip is amazingly reminiscent of this, when you regard it structurally.

Edelweiss

ay•duhl•vise *noun*

This flower, of stonking-Rodgers-and-Hammerstein-augmented fame, has a very simple etymology: edelweiss combines the German words for 'noble' *edel* with *weiss*, meaning 'white'. However, its Latin name is a far more intimate portrait. *Leontopodium* comes, originally, from the Greek *leontopódion* or 'lion's paw'. The petals of an edelweiss are not smooth, but fuzzy, and texturally resemble a lion's paw exactly.

Dandelion

dan • duh • lai • uhn noun

And lions do not stop there when it comes to floral etymology! The dandelion is a very pretty weed with its sunny bloom and has long, jaggedy leaves like a lion's teeth or, as the French would say, *dent de lion*. Say that faster and faster and what have you got?

Anemone

uh • neh • muh • nee noun

Anemones are beautiful flowers that have wide, plate-like petals and come in oodles upon oodles of cheerful colours, including crimson and magenta. They love dappled, woodland shade and typically thrive in cool and breezy spots. It's no wonder their attractive name means 'wind flower' or 'daughter of the wind' in Greek. They make their home in the spots many flowers try their best to avoid. Perhaps bestow these on an intrepid soul.

Lavender

la • vuhn • duh noun

Sometimes you get a chicken-and-egg phenomenon with words. One thinks that lavender bath products are named for the scent of the flower they contain when, in fact, *lavender* is likely named for its ubiquity in bath products. For, it is probable that the Latin *lavare*, meaning 'to wash', inspired the christening of this intensely aromatic flower, popular in scents and soaps for as long as they have existed. It is certainly omnipresent in my ablutions.

Crocus

krow • kuhs noun

As I write, these spring flowers are ubiquitous and ever cheering.

The ones I spy now are in friendly clusters and are all a vivid purple. Pretty as the blossoms are, there is an even greater appreciation for their stigmas which are dried and ground into luxurious, delicious saffron. The spice's provenance gives it its sweet, floral flavour. Saffron was a must-have spice in Greek cookery, not least because of its versatility; sublime with fish, poultry, even in cakes. Consequently, the Greek *krokos* meant both 'crocus' and 'saffron', as the celebration of the former was inextricably bound to its production of the latter.

Cyclamen

si • kluh • muhn noun

You cannot mistake these flowers. Their leaves look as though every vein has been frostbitten, and the petals seem to reach effortlessly to the skies. However distinctive their superterranean appearance, it is, like the orchid, their subterranean looks that give them their name. Their bulbs are perfect orbs that look like unwashed new potatoes. These disproportionately large, circular bulbs were probably responsible for the name that contains the *cycle* of myriad round things, from the Greek *kyklos*, meaning 'circle'. Incidentally, if you need a pronunciation guide, I always think 'sick lemon'.

Nosegay

nowz • gay noun

Here is another compound word. But this is not a compound noun since *gay*, here, is not referring to a person. Here, *gay* is an adjective akin to 'joyous'. It describes a posy, small enough for each individual flower to be detected by the olfactory nerve when hovering beneath the nose. When the nose is assaulted by this heady melange of aromas, it is made gay. No change in the nose's sexual orientation, but a nose suffused with delight at this panoply of perfume.

Tussie mussie

tuh • see muh • see *noun*

I can tell you little about the etymology of *tussie mussie*, other than it was a Victorian term for a nosegay. Its inclusion in this chapter is entirely selfish and to do with my enormous delight in saying 'tussie mussie'.

How to... talk about gender

The sad thing about progress is that it has a very spikey graph. One would expect (because of recent history where social references stop with the Victorians) that the upward trajectory is consistent and inevitable, but there were times in remoter history of greater liberation for women and queer people. You only need look at both groups' representation in the Greek myths cited in these pages. Oscar Wilde cloaked his 1880 essay about his theories of Shakespeare's 'only begetter of these ensuing sonnets Mr WH', in a short story, because even mooting his identity was perilous, whereas Shakespeare, nearly 300 years earlier wrote and published them!

Gender

jen • duh *noun*

We see presenters, who shall remain nameless, tying themselves in knots over the question of gender. They pretend to be angrily befoxed, in a cynical bid for ratings spikes, and call their feigned puzzlement journalism. It is quite simple. Gender is not, nor has it ever been, binary. The biggest clue? The word itself. It is the same word as *genre*, with identical etymology, meaning 'of a type'.

Cloudy of gender

I ping about on the gender spectrum like a yo-yo, and would be called non-binary, if I were able to accept that gender ever was. I like *cloudy of gender* as a description of one hovering above that spectrum, making it all deliciously nebulous, clouding any lines that may, arbitrarily, have been drawn on it.

Epicene

eh • puh • seen *adjective noun*

Etymologically speaking, *epicene* is one of the most neutral words concerning gender. It means 'with characteristics of all genders'. Its supreme neutrality exists because it was not originally applied to people, but words. In gendered languages, the epicene nouns were those that could fall into either gender. They were the 'common' nouns, which is where the word epicene comes from, since *koinos* is Greek for 'common'. Epicene, now, is used to describe the sort of face or frame that has something 'in common' with all genders.

Androgyny

an • droj • uh • nee *noun*

An *android* is a robot, but etymologically speaking, it is a machine in the model of a 'man' from the Greek *andro*. *Gynaecology*, (yes! I am going there), is the study of the female reproductive system, since *gyn* is 'female'. So, *androgyny* is, to my mind, a lovely word that explores having giant dollops of both male and female. My androgyny is often remarked upon, and it is something with which I feel very much at home. It seems in keeping with my personality and, I believe, helps me relate to a greater number of people.

They

Thay pronoun

The world of pronouns, if it is tricky at all, is only tricky because language is clunky. We are really all 'theys' as we all exist on the scale of endless possibilities that is gender, as described above. But he/she/they does make 'they' seem a bit like the one in the middle. A fulcrum rather than a calliper. In lieu of anything better, let us regard *they* as a calliper that can glide across the entire scale to its heart's content.

Embrace the clunk

My cousin and I, in acknowledging that a patriarchal language is unlikely to regurgitate a perfect gender fluid pronoun, have coined the phrase *embrace the clunk*. Today's coiners have to work with their existing toolbox so as not to alienate people. We must remember this if we find ourselves bemoaning the clunkiness of it. That is unequivocally the fault of the toolbox, not the coiners. In the meantime, *embrace the clunk*. Clunks, after all, disappear with practise.

Queer the pitch

The day the gay community reclaimed the word *queer*, I danced a merry jig. Not because we had an umbrella term that successfully covered LGBTQ+, but because I could give *queer the pitch* the renaissance it deserves. *Pitches* in Victorian England were allocated squares of street market where stall owners and street performer plied their trade. The pitch might be *queered* or 'skewed' by rain or competition. It became the pithiest phrase, to my knowledge, for any skewing of plans or action. I use it whenever a pitch is queered, not just because of the queering of the pitch in question but because the phrase itself has a lightness of touch that takes the sting out of the pitch queering *du jour*.

Thussy

thuh • see noun

They/them genitals are also penetrating the world of lexicons. Though I curdle at the word *pussy*, my tympanic membrane appears not to mind *thussy*. The gender fluid community is very playful with portmanteaux, although, there may be a lacuna here when it comes to they/them cock. *Thock*? We must not, I think, resort to *thick*.

'But thou, to whom my jewels trifles are, ...' says Shakespeare to his *beautiful* Mr WH in Sonnet 48. I mention it here because Shakespeare is so exquisitely unusual in his reverence for the feminine beauty in men. In fact, it is liberally scattered throughout his 154 sonnets. In Sonnet 48, he says his lover's coruscating beauty makes his jewels seem comparatively flat. In the later Sonnet 126, Shakespeare further states that his lover has done some delicious deal with nature in order to preserve his beauty:

'O thou, my lovely boy, who in thy pow'r
Dost hold time's fickle glass his sickle hour,
Who hast by waning grown, and therein show'st
Thy lovers withering, as thy sweet self grow'st' –

It is a beauty that is singular, but moreover, in terms of gender, singularly described.

Hijra

hij•ruh noun

In Western coinings concerning gender, we have busied ourselves putting a measure of both male and female *in*. Conversely, in India, they opted for a word that takes male and female *out*. *Hijra* was originally an Arabic word meaning 'departure'. *Hijras* have been revered for their departure from the polar ends of *male* and *female*. I love the notion of the *hijras'* exodus from anything binary to create their esteemed beauty.

How to... colour your emotions

My beloved nephew (and best chum) Artie is six years old. He is already attempting to charter the complex world of emotions. How do we navigate them? How do we characterise them? The simplest way may be colour. His favourite book is *The Colour Monster* by the brilliant Anna Llenas. It gives emotional states an identity through wonderful, bright colours: green is calm, red is angry, yellow is happy and so on. Artie instantly took to colouring his emotions, and it does seem to be in our global DNA to do so.

La vie en rose

lah vee ong rohz noun

I have been called a cockeyed optimist many times and by friends of many nationalities. As a result, I have learned that my 'rose-tinted spectacles', as I call them, can also be *rosarote brille* in German and *occhiali rosa* in Italian. My favourite, however, does not translate so neatly. *La vie en rose* is 'life in pink'. How divinely, romantically French that, instead of merely donning something that temporarily alters our world view, we are plunged into an existence where everything takes on a pinkish hue. The tint belongs to life itself and not to our face furniture.

From pink to red. Artie's red is for anger, but the singular Holly Golightly in Truman Capote's *Breakfast at Tiffany's* went further and coined *the mean reds*. These far surpassed the blues that she attributed to 'getting fat' and instead were reserved for that horrible, overwhelming feeling of being afraid and not knowing why.

The mean reds may trump *the blues*. You couldn't, even ironically, suffuse a smile with *mean reds*, but ...

Glas wen

glaas wen noun

The nearest translation of this untranslatable Welsh expression is a 'wry smile', but it is colour that sets this smile on the wonk. 'Glas' is Welsh for 'blue'. Blues music is littered with minor or 'blue' notes which make it sound sad so, to paint something as synonymous with happiness as a smile with the opposite emotional colour (even in Artie's book) must make that smile deeply ironic.

Chiaroscuro

kee • aa • ruh • skyuor • row noun

This Italian word means the 'light and shade'. My singing teacher used it as a helpful term for visualising the brightness of the 'head voice' and richer tones of the chest. It also serves as the perfect lexical distillation of the vast spectrum of emotional colour chartered in this chapter.

Crestfallen
krest • faw • luhn adjective

One might not instantly associate *crestfallen* with colour, but this hugely evocative word is inextricably linked to it in my own imagination. The word is a compound one: The *crest* has *fallen* in sadness or world-weariness. The animals that sport a crest, chiefly birds, typically have crests of immensely colourful plumage. I always imagine the crestfallen as regarded from behind. The approacher sees nothing more than the slumped back and nape of the neck. Devoid – figuratively and literally – of colour, for the crest, in this forlorn posture, is quite invisible.

Ghataa
gha • taa noun

Ghataa is the *scuro* end of chiaroscuro. It is Hindi for 'big grey clouds'; the grey clouds that are inclined to follow you when you are in a state of grief and will only lift when you begin to heal.

Komorebi
ko • moh • reh • bee noun

This untranslatable Japanese word combines two of Artie's colour states: yellow and green. It is the joy of sunlight as seen through the calming filter of a large green leaf; a state of happy tranquility under the great oak's canopy on a lovely sunny day.

Greenness

green • ness noun

You can, of course, be green with envy, but green*ness* is what I more often feel. This green is green as a seedling: so fresh in the world that wisdom and savvy are conspicuous in their absence. I endeavour to fly in the face of my own greenness to enrich my existence as much as possible and, hopefully, wind up a little less verdant.

Pallid

pa • luhd adjective

Pallid, from the Latin *pallidus* meaning 'pale' or 'colourless', can be used to describe the complexion but also to describe the spirit. After losing enthusiasm for a job, one might offer a pallid replica of one's former performance. I think the word is lovely for its implied temporariness. It reminds me of the way in which blades of grass store their greenness below the surface when the sun is at its most powerful, looking very sorry. But the sequestered green will flood the blade again once it rains.

Feuillemorte

fuy • eh • morte adjective

Yellow sunlight may also shine through a dead leaf which, etymologically, is the French *feuillemorte*. Nature's sepia, if you like. A feuillemorte tint is a romantic one, perhaps tinged with sadness. These complex colour mixings describe multiple emotional outlooks or states. They are relatively recent takes on nuanced feelings. But what about the extremes? For that, we must consult the etymologist and the doctor.

How to... identify emotional overload

If life is full of fret, I am fretful as all get-out ... If life is devoid of fret, I shall conjure something to fret about.

Fretful as a porcupine

I use the phrase *fretful as a porcupine* a great deal because the porcupine's panic behaviour is such a good example of adrenaline-induced bodily turbo drive. When threatened, the noble creature stamps its feet, grunts and erects every available quill. Every cell is charged in a bid to deter and protect.

Fret not nor fear

My father has so many words and phrases in which he takes such visible delight. This is the one I associate most with his role in family life. He is the lone pragmatist and only successful mollifier in the family. Two of his three children are fretters by nature. Maybe because this sweet phrase, that I have only ever heard him utter, has danced on my tympanic membrane since I was knee-high to a grasshopper, it creates instant comfort.

Melancholy

meh • luhng • ko • lee adjective noun

Melan is the Greek root meaning 'black'. It is therefore perfectly logical that it should find its way into *melanin*, the dark pigment in one's hair and skin. But to discover its route into *melancholia* or sadness, one has to go all the way back to 'the father of medicine', Hippocrates, who stated that humans are comprised of four liquids that determine our emotional states. He called these liquids 'the humours'. They were blood, yellow bile, black bile and phlegm. The black bile was responsible for human sadness, so melancholy simply means an excess of this black bile. I think what Hippocrates really hit upon was how palpable profound sadness and depression can be. Depression for years was referred to by medics as *melancholia* and the allusion to a very physical black spectre was

ELEUTHEROPHOBIA

uh·loo·thuh·ruh·fow·bee·uh *noun*

A fear of freedom. A phobia many of us never thought we would know but did after the lockdowns. For some, acclimatising to limited freedom proved easier than the reintroduction of freedom.

popularised again by Winston Churchill, who referred to his depression as his 'black dog'. For those of you less inclined to nuance and subtlety in emotional discourse, we must move away from colour. If it is extremes you are after, there is always ...

Immanent

i • muh • nuhnt *adjective*

Though much of this book deals with the world without, this chapter deals exclusively with the world within. Our *immanent* world. This does not mean, like its homophone *imminent*, a coming-soon world, but the world that 'dwells within'. The Latin *manere* means 'to dwell', and gives us a word that is a more literal 'dwelling', a *manor*.

Ecstasy

ek • stuh • see *noun*

Ek is the Greek root meaning 'out of'. Most of its children have a fairly clear hereditary line: *appendectomy* is the cutting out of the appendix, *eccentric* is out of the centre or 'norm' and – slightly more tenuously – *eclectic* is 'picking out' of art, style or thought of divergent origins. But *ecstasy*? A transcendent state that is both euphoric and metaphysical. How do we reach that? Incidentally, I am not asking for a trip, merely an etymological route. Ecstasy is a 'putting out' of one's mind. So, we really are talking about a cognitive transcendence. The notion of the mind living 'out of' the body when in this state. Boy! Those Greeks knew a thing or two.

Enthusiasm

uhn • thyoo • zee • a • zm *noun*

Theos is the Greek root meaning 'God'. A *theist*, therefore, is a 'god' or 'gods' believer and an *atheist* believes in none. *Enthusiasm* is more imaginative. Etymologically, it is 'god inside you', and it is not nearly as sacrilegious as it sounds. It really means approaching something with an almost divine zeal, as though divinity is in one's very cells! This is not that Holy Spirit/Virgin Mary-esque corporeal take over. Think osmosis, not penetration.

Hysteria

huh • steeuh • ree • uh *noun*

Hystera is the Greek root meaning 'womb' or 'uterus'. Naturally, the womb root birthed medical descendants like *hysterectomy*, the 'cutting out' of the womb. But hysteria? A giddy, unravelled emotional state. What has this to do with all things uterine? We are in the world of linguistic skeuomorph, when time, knowledge and social mores march on but language refuses to do so. The word, regrettably, means 'womb sickness'. So, hysterical behaviour was something so-called physicians attributed (with complete conjecture) to the uterus. It stuck. But luckily the etymology is largely forgotten.

Ignominy

ig • nuh • muh • nee *noun*

Nomin is the Latin root meaning 'name'. It is in many logical offshoots, namely (see what I did there) *misnomer*, which is a name given that is malapropos. Method actors might argue that 'acting' is a misnomer, as they feel they are often *living* the role. *Nominate*, originally meant to *name* someone in order to put them forward. But *ignominy*? What has abject humiliation to do with names? The literal meaning here is 'without name', so the link really refers to the possible loss of one's status, and even title, in the event of an ignominious debacle.

Remorse

ruh • maws noun

Mordere is the Latin word meaning 'to bite'. This root found itself masticating life's lunacies in the word *mordancy*, a sharp and 'biting' style. With even more lucidity, it can be found in *morsel* or 'little bite'. But *remorse*? What has contrition to do with biting? If broken down, it is simply and metaphorically a 'biting back', which is a very nifty and wonderfully physical description of precisely what the conscience does. We often talk of the conscience pricking us, but biting feels more befitting.

Bonjour Tristesse

bon • zhuo tris • tès noun

Here is my favourite emotional idiom. We colour emotions, but some writers have gone further still and personified them. Françoise Sagan's 1954 novel personified *tristesse* or 'sadness' in its title by greeting her. When, four years later, the hugely successful Deborah Kerr film of the same name came out, the phrase was further popularised. I particularly like the surreal use of *bonjour*, which is literally 'good day', and, logically, should be a greeting ascribed to happiness but generates bizarre poetic irony when applied to sadness.

How to...
dodge offence
(while speaking
your mind)

The question is, I find, does my need to say this supersede my desire not to offend? If so (and these instances are rare), it becomes a question of how to frame the remark. Mercifully, we Brits live in the global capital of euphemism, a hotbed of word creation, and, in addition, hoovered the world's lexicon when there are holes in our own. Our creative tools, therefore, are rich and varied. Here are a few happenstances where you might need them ...

Don't make a nest in it

One of the trickiest things I find, as an erstwhile thespian, is going to a play at the behest of a dear chum and not being wild about it. One has to pay a visit backstage and some form of praise must be imparted. Truthfully, I can count on the fingers of one hand the times this has been the case since, more often than not, I am bedazzled. What will happen frequently, though, is that you spot one chink, the omission of which might help beyond measure if you could only find the words to tactfully highlight it. Cue the master of the backstage note, the late Alan Rickman. He adored his *Truly, Madly, Deeply* co-star Juliet Stevenson and would devotedly attend her stage work. Stevenson has said that typically one dreads notes from fellow actors, but Rickman's were brilliantly original and staggeringly useful. Her favourite? 'Don't make a nest in it.' This was his caveat for what he regarded as an exceptionally fine performance but with the faintest trace of getting too comfy. Stevenson carries the caveat to this day, even electing (as I witnessed with amazement) to toss a coin on stage every night in *Mary Stuart* to see which actor would play Mary and which would play Elizabeth I. Absence of nest? Absence of tree!

Avert

uh • vuht verb

This chapter is all about *averting*: averting offence, averting conflict, averting disaster. To avert is, etymologically speaking, to 'turn off' course before going headlong into some unwanted situation. *Vertere* is Latin for 'to turn' and this matriarch root has given us many children: *invert* 'to turn in', thereby taking the opposing view, *introvert*, 'to turn within', so as to retreat from the world, and *extrovert* 'to turn outside', so that the individual is most entertained by activities outside of their internal life.

It's no one I know!

Sticking with the theatre briefly, what do you say when a zestful set designer shows you the set of your new play, and you discover the centrepiece is a giant phallus? Coral Browne, never at a loss for words, calmly sized up the swollen golden (non cast member's) member and at last determined 'Well, it's no one I know.'

Oh!

A dear friend of mine, a Mr Ouzerdine, once said to me my life's vocal score consisted of approximately four octaves of 'oh's'. I find 'oh' the most brilliantly useful word for discourse lubrication, particularly in awkward moments. When somebody says something politically outré, I opt for an extended growled basso 'ohhhh' with a tilted head, which seems to say a great deal without saying anything. When presented with a newborn, I find involuntary 'oh's' glissando up an octave, accompanied by a smile and a vocal fry. When somebody is brusque and I am suffering from *treppenwitz* (*see* page 31) I will at least have the wits to show instant displeasure with a high sticcatto 'oh!'. When with my various sproglets, and wanting to convey disappointment without labouring the point, I employ a penetrative gaze, drop the shoulders and the larynx for a cello-voiced, descending 'oh'. Conversely, when the sproglets evince delight, a shorter, brighter, major keyed 'oh!' leaps out of me.

Oh Christmas!

Granny, the matriarch of meteorological hyperbole (*see* page 82), endeavours to eschew fruity Anglo-Saxon four-letter words. She is largely, though not completely, successful. Grandpa was a lifelong Francophile and they would stay in a small studio apartment in Dieppe where we would occasionally join them. There was one rather overstuffed cupboard in this apartment containing cloths, dusters, a mop, a broom, brushes, buckets, polish, detergents and countless other things. Towards the end of our visit, Granny, who is adept at a scurryfunge (a magnificent word for a rapid tidy), opened that most useful cupboard. Out fell the entire contents. Her face went puce, I can almost remember steam proceeding from her ears. We all waited with excitement to see which forbidden word would follow Granny's growled 'Ohhhhhh ...' It was, disappointingly, 'Christmas'. I was very au fait with 'crumbs' and 'fiddlesticks', but this was new and, I thought, a graduation. Was it the insertion of *Christ*, however innocuously, that did it? It took the straining of every sinew not to dissolve into giggles.

Etymology is your friend ...

Brexit is two things: the most polarising domestic political subject and the most-used portmanteau of recent years. It is amazing how successfully one can sidestep the former by focusing on the latter, especially when looking to other European portmanteaux, or possible portmanteaux, in the cast of Brexit: *Frexit* is perhaps a more attrative portmanteau than Brexit, but *Itaxit*? Sounds more like a radical fiscal idea that a political possibility. And let's hope Latvia does not leave, since *Latexit* is already a kink movement and could lead to all kinds of confusion.

I zigged when I should have zagged

What does one say in that awkward moment of meeting a perfect stranger in a doorway or an aisle and both of you aim for the unoccupied space on the same side? What if you then, in an attempt to rectify the situation, both aim for the unoccupied space on the opposite side? This could go on interminably without some sort of gesture or discourse. Fellow idiom collector, the incomparably brilliant Alan Bennett, was met with this awkward jerky hover in a shop in Manhattan. His opposite number's response was so delicious he recorded it in his diary that evening: 'I'm so sorry! I zigged when I should have zagged.'

I'm so sorry, I'm down to a diatribe a month

I suppose the other intensely polarising subject of our age is Covid-19. Vaccinations, mask wearing, policy, domestic behaviour all have created and, in some cases, continue to create, polarisation. A dear, dear friend of mine is an anti-vaxxer. I didn't know until I dined with her recently. I took my Pfizer-infused cells along with me, of course – we go everywhere together. We had a marvellous time, with the notable exception of a ten-minute anti-vaccination soliloquy, during which I ate and listened hard for a gossamer thread that might lead to another topic. About three weeks later, I had a birthday and suppered with another chum. To my astonishment, he began to do the same. I, alas, have one of those faces that says 'convert me'. This time, I felt less inclined to listen, so I said, 'I'm so sorry. Three weeks ago I listened to a very hefty soliloquy on this topic. I'm now limiting myself to a diatribe a month.' After a pregnant pause it seemed to do the trick, and the shank of the evening was as congenial as the start.

Sollocks!

so • luhks noun

Fight de-escalation. If the above does not work and you inadvertently insult an actor after a performance, put a name to the phallus, your 'oh's' strike the wrong note, you bungle your etymology, you insist on zagging, or you get drawn into Covid combat, you might need a de-escalator. This brings me to Noël

Coward and *Private Lives*. I shall sketch the plot. Erstwhile spouses Amanda and Elyot are honeymooning with their new spouses Victor and Sybil. Unfortunately, they are in adjacent suites. On moonlit neighbouring balconies, Amanda and Elyot fall in love all over again, forgetting what once drove them apart: their spats. When they start to quarrel anew, they decide the only answer is a mutually agreed de-escalation word. It should be quick, memorable and funny – an instant diffuser. The word is *sollocks*. Sollocks proves to be wonderfully efficient in Act I, but its power depreciates as the play rolls on. Nevertheless, I can think of no better word for spat-zapping.

'Enough is as good as a feast'

Mary Poppins is endlessly quotable. Some of her finest utterances are those where she is engaged in tricky verbal combat. On the verge of being sacked, she cleverly takes Mr Banks's melody, sings it back to him but cleaved to her own words and, before you know it, instead of a P45 she has an extra day off with pay. At her next upbraiding, Mr Banks demands an explanation. He is succinctly told, 'I *never* explain *anything*.' Some of the strongest protestations she faces come from the children. When she does permit a kicking up of heels, she is very definite about when one's heels should firmly reconnect with the floor. The children long to eke out the fun, but Mary Poppins answers, 'Enough is as good as a feast.' So true is this aphorism, one cannot contest.

How to... describe all your corporeal bits and juices

Every contour of your body is important. Consequently, at some stage they will have been christened, nicknamed, or both. Our bodies with their manifold knobbly bits, each with a bespoke appellation, are magnificent simply as fleshy masses. But then consider all their magic tricks: secreting, diffusing, emitting, signalling – whether we want them to or not! Barely an hour goes by without our mentioning either a bit or a juice, either literally or figuratively. It is time to admire some of our protrusions and secretions, and their impact on our discourse.

Callipygian

ka • luh • pi • gee • uhn *adjective*

This word comes from the seventeenth century, at a time when the divinely contoured Doric sculptures were all the rage in Britain. The Brits took the Greek *kallos* for 'beauty' and *pyge*, 'buttocks', and made a portmanteau. *Callipygian* described perhaps the most substantial, arresting contours on these statues. Thus, 'beautiful buttocks', lightly draped in classical etymology, entered the vernacular in the upper echelons of society.

Whiffles

wiff • uhlz *noun*

In the introduction to this chapter, I mention bits and juices. There's an omission there, I'm afraid, for this word is neither. It is a corporeal state. *Whiffles* is Francis Grose's word for full scrotal relaxation as documented in *The Dictionary of the Vulgar Tongue* (1811). This was Grose's Georgian compendium of all the words that might not have made Samuel Johnson's earlier and more formal dictionary but were liberally used in the inns and taverns of the day. The state is apt to occur when very warm, relaxed, or both.

Malleolus

muh • lee • uh • luhs *noun*

The late seventeenth century was a good time for christening our unchristened bits. Have you ever wondered what those protruding knobs either side of your ankles are called? Wonder no more. *Malleoli* look rather like someone has inserted a hammer in your leg and the two faces of its head are poking out. It appears that those that named them felt the same, since *malleus* is the Latin word for 'hammer'. Incidentally, *malleus* also gives us the word 'mallet'!

Bathykolpian

baa • theey • kol • pyan *adjective*

One for the ample-bosomed. The ample-pecced may also qualify as *bathykolpians* – etymologically speaking. This is because the word is more about that deep groove between those fleshy bits than the bits themselves. The Greek gives us *bathys* meaning 'deep' and *kolpos* meaning 'breast'. The 'depth' refers to that sternummy bit where rivulets of sweat might run or necklaces might dangle.

Cervix

sur • viks *noun*

Cervix is the Latin root meaning 'neck'. If you are familiar with the spinal curves: coccyx, sacral, lumbar, thoracic, cervical, you will know that the last is the uppermost curve and concerns the bones that make up the neck. What on earth has the neck to do with the passage at the end of the uterus we call the cervix? The cervix was originally the 'neck' of any organ that had a large neck-like passage. Over time, cervix gained a special uterine exclusivity.

Glabella

gluh • bel • uh *noun*

In just the same way *novella* tells us we are talking about a 'little novel', *glabella* tells us we are talking about a 'little glaber'. What is a *glaber* when it's at home? It is, in Latin, a 'bald' spot. As I write, I can almost hear you protest at the vaguery, as we have oodles of those on our bodies: our *weenus*, for example (the bald, fleshy, tuggable bit covering our elbow – see next entry), our mastoids and the balls – wait for it – of our feet. But this *ella* is smaller than any of those. The glabella refers to that tiny bald spot between the eyebrows!

Weenus

wee • nuhs noun

It has an entry of its own principally for pronunciation purposes. *Weenus* should rhyme with *penis*. If you feel this word sounds a little too naughty for polite society, you may wish to rename it the *glabella major*, since it is also a small bald spot. Just not quite as small as the dinky *glabella*.

Nausea

naw • zee • uh noun

Naus is the Greek root meaning 'ship'. It sails jolly neatly into *nautical*, or 'pertaining to ships'. *Naus* is also found in the word *astronaut*, a sailor of the stars (which I think is rather beautiful). But *nausea*? You can see how sickness might be related to ships, but isn't it a little tenuous? The coining of this word was specifically inspired by awful, stomach-churning seasickness. Subsequently, the word found ubiquity on land as well as sea.

Eructation

eruk • tay • shn noun

Here is a rather elegant sounding synonym for a burp. You may argue that, given the title of this chapter, an eructation is technically neither a bit nor a juice. However, beyond it being a lovely word (in my opinion), I have an etymological justification for its inclusion here. *Eructare* is the Latin meaning to 'belch forth', and thus, partially vomit. Strictly speaking, an eructation is the breed of burp that has the tiniest hint of sick in it.

yo·nik *adjective*

The word for anything
reminiscent of the vulva,
from whorls of blooms to
snug cashmere sleeves.

Lineament

lin • ee • uh • muhnt noun

I might know you by your facial and bodily *lineaments*. These are the distinguishing lines of your face and frame, from the Latin *linea*, meaning 'thread or line'. Your profile might be equally useful for recognition, and draws on the same theme since *filum* is 'thread', and the singular line of your lineaments is fine and threadlike.

Dexterity

dek • steh • ruh • tee noun

Dexter is the Latin root meaning 'on the right'. Understandable then (although insulting to the left-handed) that *ambidextrous* literally means 'having two right hands'. Did you spot the implied prejudice? Not two equally able hands but two *right* hands. Sadly, for the left-handed among us, the Romans believed right-handedness was inextricably linked to superior skill. So much so, that dexterity, which etymologically is simply 'right-handedness', quickly evolved to mean skilfulness. Occasionally, one feels that when the scribes finally immortalised these words on parchment they could have done with, if you'll pardon the pun, a hand!

Yonic

yo • nik adjective

From the Sanskrit *yoni*, meaning 'vulva'. When Jo Brand guested on my word-centric podcast, she pointed out that the word 'clitoris' was entirely absent from *Gray's Anatomy*, published in 1858, but the penile study therein was extensive. She further noted, if you were to play orgasm *Top Trumps*, the clitoris, with its 8,000 nerve endings, would trounce the penis with its meagre 4,000. Similarly, in language, we describe almost any proud, extended protrusion as phallic (at least I do – sorry to tar you with my smut brush). But do we even know the equivalent? *Yonic.* The yonic whorl of a bloom, the yonic cleave of a valley, the yonic enveloping of a snug turtleneck.

Baculum

ba • kyuh • luhm noun

Baculum can be traced all the way back to the Greek *baklon*, meaning 'stick'. It is, if you like, the stick within the penis, or penis bone, which oh-so-mercifully we male humans do not have. In the animal kingdom, however, there are many as the red panda, snow leopard and meerkat will attest. In the same way *boner* must have been coined, there have been a couple of observational moments where I have heard a little internal voice say, 'Gosh! That's as proud as a baculum!'

Gravid

gra • vuhd noun

Gravis is the Latin root meaning 'heavy'. So, if one wishes to discuss an issue of *gravity*, then it is likely to be an issue of immense weight. Similarly, a person with *gravitas* carries social weight; dignity and command. A thinner etymological thread – certainly a finer cord than the umbilical – gives us *gravid*, meaning pregnant. You may have guessed that the missing link is the added weight of eggs or a foetus to the animal and human bodies. It means 'heavy with child'. The word is a relic of a time when the gravid were only truly detectable (paused menstruation aside) at the stage of pregnancy when one is heavier or more visibly carrying.

Insulin

in • syuh • luhn noun

Insula is the Latin root meaning 'island'. Unlike an island, the root has clear pathways across the seas of etymological mystery to her siblings. *Peninsula* is perhaps the most obvious as it is a 'near-island', a piece of land jolly nearly – but not quite – surrounded by water. *Insular* is similarly clear, it means 'island-like' or isolated. But *insulin*? It might make more sense if you have heard of the 'Islands of Langerhans'; not a sunny equatorial resort, but regions of the pancreas discovered in 1869 by esteemed German anatomist, Paul Langerhans. These island-like (you see!) regions of the organ secrete a juice that became known simply as the island substance, or insulin!

Oestrogen

ee • struh • jn noun

Oistros is the Greek root meaning 'gadfly'. The gadfly, for beasts of the field, is a most annoying insect that bites their flesh, often inducing a brief spell of 'hysteria' (*see* page 57). 'Ah!' you might cavil, 'so we're back to that,' and I'm afraid you would be right. The misogyny bug bites our words with all the vigour of the gadfly. For, this hysteria in animals was what (male) language creators felt they saw in women during hormonal spikes, hence oestrogen. Sometimes I cannot help feeling one is less likely to get bitten by lexical gadfly if one ignores etymology altogether. Oh no! We are in the wrong book for that.

Serotonin

seh • ruh • tow • nuhn noun

I think you are going to like this one. Serotonin is that glorious hormone that helps cognitive function, mood and memory.

Many people call it our 'happy hormone'. The word itself combines two very familiar words, *serum*, which means 'watery fluid' and *tonic*, which means 'that which promotes good health'. Sometimes etymology reveals such a neat coining that it covers all facets of a multifaceted thing in just four short syllables. This particular watery fluid, especially these days, is arguably the ultimate tonic.

Prurient

pruor • ree • uhnt adjective

Prurire is the Latin root meaning 'to itch'. This itchy root becomes chronic in the skin condition prurigo. But *prurient*? How exactly does excessive interest in the sexual and the crude connect to itching? Itching, incidentally, is all that prurient means, etymologically speaking. It is the notion that those naughty, base thoughts that tap dance incessantly in one's grey matter (that we are all familiar with) are 'itch-like'. They are persistent unless scratched.

Splenetic

spluh • neh • tuhk adjective

Poor old spleen. This organ has had a bad rap since the sixteenth century. In those days, if you were extremely bad tempered you might be described as *spleenful*. *Splenetic* is an ever-so-slightly more attractive transmutation of spleenful. It goes back to the humours again, since the spleen was thought to be the chief black bile squirter in our corporeal system (*see* page 54). Cod medicine. Mind you, you might not have the sunniest countenance with a grumbling spleen.

Choleric

ko • luh • ruhk *adjective*

Another humour-inspired temperament. From the Greek *khole*, meaning 'bile'. This bile is not the black bile of the spleen, but the yellow bile of the liver. This disposition is less consistently morose, à la splenetic, and more inclined to wild outbursts. In fact, the choleric type is far more likely to create acute anxiety in whomever flanks them, as people of this nature are entirely unpredictable.

Manipulate

muh • ni • pyoo • layt *verb*

Manus is the Latin root meaning 'hand'. A mere handspan away, of course, is *manually* or 'by hand' and, equally close at hand (sorry! Always handy with a pun. Oh crumbs!) *manicure* or 'care of the hands'. What about *manipulate*? We tend to regard manipulation as far less tangible and more of an emotional/ intellectual persuasiveness. Originally it was exclusively physical: 'to shape with one's hands' and, over time, waxed metaphorical. It came to describe a similar sort of fashioning of events, situations or people, where one's wits or wiles take the place of one's hands.

Up to the oxters

There's nothing particularly prepossessing about an armpit. You may, therefore, regard the unattractive word as apropos for its subject. *Oxter*, however, is another matter. This lovely word comes from the Old English *oxta* and is rare, to say the least, in my pocket of the United Kingdom. In Scotland, however, especially in the north-east, it is an enormously popular synonym. So much so, that our southern, 'I'm up to me armpits at the moment,' referring to our level of busyness as though occupation were a liquid reaching a certain corporeal height, has become 'Up to my oxters!'

Autopsy

aw • top • see *noun* *verb*

Opsis is the Greek root meaning 'sight'. It sees its way (did you spot that one?) neatly into *optical*, which means pertaining to sight, and *myopia*, which is 'short-sightedness'. But *autopsy*? How the dickens does a post-mortem connect to the aforementioned? Autopsy really means a 'seeing first-hand', the only way to ingest the nuanced information the corpse will offer the probing eye. Next time you hear Jessica Fletcher ask to be present at one in *Murder, She Wrote*, remember that the word itself is more concerned with Jessica's retinas than the poor old Cabot Cove corpse!

How to... talk euphemistically about the bathroom

The loo, the bog, the john, the can. A very necessary room. A room that apparently, over a lifetime, we occupy for around 92 days. Anything else to which we dedicated 92 days of our lives we would probably talk about. But this is the home of our smelliest creations. Our least prepossessing leakages. So, it will forever be shrouded in euphemism but, as these pages strongly argue, euphemisms can be as delicious as the things they are masking are not.

The powder room

Euphemisms for going to the loo are endless. One of the most famous of yesteryear is 'going to the powder room'. It was especially popular in 1920s America, where cocaine was wildly popular. Naturally, 90 per cent of women using this euphemism would do so with exclusive reference to face powder, but the two-pronged nature of this euphemism would not have been lost on someone like the late, great Tallullah Bankhead, who would always take both powders on her loo trips. Of her penchant for powder she famously said, 'Cocaine isn't habit forming. I should know, I've been using it for years.' As an addendum, I must say, I never go to the powder room without powder of the classic variety ... so I'd like to stretch this euphemism, like knicker elastic, to the powder room's neighbouring little boy's room.

The fourth

I have a podcast all about words which is a true labour of love (excuse this minuscule plug but it is called *Tom Read Wilson Has Words With ...*). I interview guests through the prism of their language: apropos their pocket(s) of the world, their work, even their coinings. My favourite guests tend to be comedians because they are the most liberal coiners. Jennifer Saunders is responsible for the *fourth*, meaning, curiously, a poo! Her grandfather was a Cambridge don. There were three major academic buildings in his college, and a fourth, much smaller erection, housed an outdoor loo. 'Going to the fourth', therefore, became a euphemism for popping to the loo. As words are apt to do, it evolved in the Saunders household to mean the larger deposit left in the loo. Going to the fourth became doing a fourth.

Horse

haws *noun*

In addition to Jennifer, I had her effulgent partner in crime, Dawn French, on the podcast. She, too, had a bathroom euphemism. Her family holidays were often spent on barges without loos. It was therefore important to take a sizeable tin bucket for family deposits. *Horse* became a two-pronged fork. When shouted loudly and extendedly, it would mask the din of wee-on-tin. It also was in recognition of the power of that din being akin to the emissions of a racehorse.

Jobbie

joh•bee *noun*

Poo is seldom effective in a love letter but in this case, I intend it to be, to my dear friend, Amanda McLaren. I have amassed a great many Scottish chums in my life, and I am invariably tickled by their piquant, comedic coinings. Amanda would quite proudly announce that she was 'off for a jobbie' which initially foxed me. Eventually, she clarified that this was a bathroom visit, specifically concerning poo. I was perplexed by this. I said it cast aspersions on the ease of her bowel movements since it sounded like it was 'a job' to get it out. She assured me that although the etymology might support my concerns, her bowel movements were regular and magnificent. I was delighted!

To make coins

In my twelve years as a Stockwellian (near Brixton in south-west London) I oft frequented a cafe adjacent to my gym. There was an enchanting Italian barista called Andrea with whom I would chat most days. One day I zipped past him, powder room bound. He stopped me in my tracks and said 'Eh, Tom? Where you go?' and on idiotic autopilot I replied, 'Just to spend a penny.' Andrea smiled his beautiful smile and said, 'What does it mean?' And I dutifully explained. The following day, there I was again, ensconced, with my iced black Americano, when I felt a tap on my shoulder. It was Andrea: 'Eh, Tom, guess where I go!' I had quite forgotten our exchange of the previous day so I said, 'Gosh! I don't know.' Andrea twinkled at me and said 'I go ... to make coins!'

The john

For a long time, and certainly for my grandparents' generation, 'the john' was an extremely popular euphemism for the loo. It is highly likely this goes back to naughty Sir John Harington, Queen Elizabeth I's 'saucy godson'. He was the author of some pretty racy poetry and *A New Discourse upon a Stale Subject: The Metamorphosis of Ajax*. This really is euphemism gone mad. We are unpicking 'john', a euphemism; John's title contains another one for loo, 'ajax', and for poo, 'stale subject'. The book, using the machinations of the flushing loo, and poo as thin veneer, was in fact a study of *political* shittiness. The notoriety of this text, and Sir John's association with the flushing loo, meant the john was destined to become a long-lasting bathroom euphemism.

Necessarium

neh • suh • seh • ree • uhm noun

We have the monks to thank for this. It is from the Latin *necesse*, meaning 'unavoidable'. Which room is uniquely unavoidable? The one designed for the unstoppable leakages and deposits that punctuate our days. The monks certainly were not aiming to tickle but, to me, the knitting of the 'unavoidable' and unwanted break from prayer into the monastic name for a loo never fails to amuse me.

Xylospongium

zai • luh • spuhnj • ee • uhm noun

Xylon of *xylophone* 'wood choir' fame, is the Greek for 'wood'. This, combined with *spongos*, meaning 'sponge', give us *xylospongium*. Sadly, this 'sponge on a stick', a forerunner of loo paper, was a shared instrument in public lavatories. Mercifully, close at hand, was a large bucket of vinegar. Demonstrating exemplary hygiene, you would dunk your soiled xylospongium in that. The stick part would outjut, ready for one's post-defecation neighbour's employment.

Lavatory

la • vuh • tuh • ree noun

The most interesting thing to me about the lav, or 'washroom' from the Latin *lavare* 'to wash', is her surprising family tree. Her sister 'lavender' is so called because the bloom was so popular in the world of ablutions. Her sister 'lavish' is even more surprising: it is, etymologically, a 'washing down' of luxuries or treasures. A deluge of delights.

Dejecta

duh • jek • tuhd noun

From the Latin *dejacta*, meaning 'that which is cast out', *dejecta* may feel *dejected*, as it has become an umbrella term for all our secretions and excretions. We may visit the loo to mop our brow, blow our nose, poo, wee, upchuck and generally leak from every orifice. It is rather an attractive word when you consider its sole purpose is to describe all our bodily gunk.

How to... follow Mrs Higgins's advice and talk about the weather

You may be reading this book in a country with barely perceptible seasons, or in a place that knows far greater meteorological extremes than I could imagine. This book was written entirely in London. The skies above my busy fingers are ever-changing and, sadly, inclined to leak. Outside under an awning, my digits have felt the sun's rays, the tickle of zephyrs, the chill of the air and even the spatter from falling raindrops while writing these pages. With such indecisiveness overhead, no wonder we have such colourful idioms where the weather is concerned.

Absolute stair rods!

My granny, my only living grandparent, is perhaps the most quotable of all my relatives. She has a tendency toward the hyperbolic, especially where the weather is concerned. A relatively modest downpour is apt to prompt either the line, 'Well, we can't possibly go out in that, it's absolute stair rods!' because the rain is no longer falling in unthreatening droplets but, to the naked eye, forming rod-like configurations as it combines through power and velocity on its way to the ground. If the heavens have really opened, then Granny will graduate to, 'Well, at least the garden will be thankful. It's pitch forks!'

Desperately in need of a roof!

We are, as a nation, of course famous for our 'stair rod' weather. When great luminaries of the performing arts have gone to Hollywood, they have often been seduced by the Californian climate. Hermione Gingold, of *Gigi* and *A Little Night Music* fame was one such star. She waxed gleeful about the perpetual sunshine of her adoptive home, and although she missed England for myriad reasons, the weather proved prohibitive. She once uttered the immortal phrase, 'England is a lovely country, but desperately in need of a roof!'

Blow winds and crack your cheeks

Because we are blessed with temperamental skies, it is not uncommon for us to personify the weather. King Lear, the eponymous character of Shakespeare's play, does it here as he challenges the tempest to do its worst: 'Blow winds and crack your cheeks!' I suppose the notion of the wind puffing out his cheeks as far as they will go, when issuing a big blow, goes all the way back to the Ancient Greeks and their god of the wind, Zephyr.

HELIOSPURRED

hee·lee·oh·spuhd *adjective, verb*

My own portmanteau for the
feeling of being charged and
galvanised by sunshine.

Rainbow weather

I like to put a PR spin on these ever-changing skies of ours. If it's a day of zipping in and out of shop doorways as sunbeams alternate with welkin leakage, I look to the quite possible consequential rainbow and refer to all the vacillations that precede it as 'rainbow weather'. Goodness knows, if a rainbow does eventually grace the skies, that's a handsome payoff for the meteorological uncertainty.

Make the western welkin blush

Speaking of *welkins*, which are, quite simply, skies, how does one describe a dallying sun that continues to warm as it paints the sky pink, refusing to go to bed. Once again, Shakespeare is both handy and untoppable. In *King John*, Lewis says:

> The sun of heaven methought was loath to set,
> But stay'd and made the western welkin blush.

I can *feel* it, so visceral is the imagery.

Clement

kle • muhnt adjective

Can you hear the faint pealing of the bells of St Clement's from the nursery rhyme of your youth? Me too. The saint it was named for was also a pope. Clement felt just right as a papal appellation since the Latin *clementem* means 'mild' or 'gentle'. *Clement* used to be an adjective far more associated with people in the days of the popes (yes – more than one!) of that name. Now, however, it is a word inspired by warm air and clear skies. On such days, a hundred or more happy voices, including my own, will chorus 'Ah! What clement weather!'

Pluviophile

ploo • vee • oh • file *noun*

Most of us favour a clement day, but there is a romance to the *pluvius*, Latin for 'rain'. Audrey Hepburn, in *Sabrina*, tells Humphrey Bogart he must only visit Paris in the rain. She explains that the chestnut trees that line her streets emit their heady perfume when it rains. That is the most romantic and intoxicating time to find yourself in Paris's bosom. For my part, there are times when I enjoy a pelt of pluvius against the window.

Freezing the balls off brass monkeys

This idiom has puzzled many. There has been many an imaginative conjuring of ornamental, betesticled brass monkeys losing their balls in the frigid air. In fact, a brass monkey is a nautical rack for storing cannon balls. Brass is apt to contract more than even anatomical balls in very chilly weather and, as a result, cannon balls were quite likely to drop off the newly shrunken rack. In a way, the balls are 'frozen off'.

Zephyrous

zeh • fuh • rus *adjective*

I seldom say 'windy', not least because it can be confused with bouts of severe flatulence. Typically, I opt for *zephyrous*. Zephyr, Greek God of the Breeze, rather blotted his copy book with me when he blew Apollo's discus off course, killing Hyacinthus (more on this egregious act in *How to say it with flowers*, page 34). However, I adore his kinder collaboration with spouse, Flora, Goddess of Flowers, where he would scoop her upon the breeze to disseminate her seedlings all over the countryside. Talk about a dream team.

How to...
have fun with
collective
nouns

Collective nouns are inherently fun. They are a game: spot the commonality. A *flamboyance* of flamingos, for have you ever met one that isn't? A *quiver* of arrows – it couldn't be a *bullseye* of arrows when so many miss. A *parliament* of owls, since, like parliament (in theory), there ought not to be one without a wise head. A *garland* of sonnets, whose literary petals unfurl from line to line. A *tower* of giraffes, a *wriggle* of worms and a *bloat* of hippos because, well ... Now we know the rules of the game, why don't we fashion some for other collectives?

A DAZZLE OF DRAG QUEENS

An appropriately spangly collective noun for the doyennes of drag.

A cadenza of sopranos

One of the collective traits of the soprano repertoire is the *cadenza*, a thrilling flourish that tends to take place at the end of an aria. They are electric. They make every cell oscillate, particularly in the knickers. Whether you are a Wagnerian soprano or favour Gilbert and Sullivan, you will have belted out a cadenza or seven.

A C of tenors

C what I did there? From lyric tenor to dramatic, there is one qualification you must have to be part of this esteemed group. You must have, in your arsenal, a thrilling High C. This, if you have ever menaced a keyboard, is the C two above middle C. In a trained tenor voice, they will have a measure of chest sound and a measure of glorious heady 'ring' in their High Cs. It will sound full voiced, as opposed to the lighter falsetto. The High C is so crucial that when Placido Domingo lost his, he switched to a baritone repertoire.

An erection of architects

Stylistically divergent and singular in approach, it is hard to find much that links the work of, say, Christopher Wren and Frank Gehry. The only thing I can think of is that they both build *up*. In other words, the link between architects of every hue, is that they preside over erections.

A flex of personal trainers

Now, this seems obvious but, I think, it is doubly fitting etymologically speaking. *Flectere* is the Latin, meaning 'to bend', which gives us the *flex* of muscles when fully contracted and pumped, but also *flexible*, meaning 'able to bend easily' or *bendy*. A good personal trainer will try and maintain their client's flexibility while maximising their flex!

A grind of baristas

The ubiquity of baristas has been overlooked by the common noun. They are brilliant in their speed and artistry. For me, the greatest thrill in the process is the grind of the bean. It emits that heady aroma that hits you the moment you cross the threshold of a coffee shop.

A snuffle of tapirs

Next to majestic giraffes, these are my favourite creatures. They look like pimped-up pigs but are, in fact, closer relations of the rhino and the zebra. They are eco-engineers who snuffle seeds and then disseminate them in their rich homemade manure: their poo. Sadly, these super gardeners of remarkable beauty are endangered.

A dazzle of drag queens

I was contemplating a *spangle* of drag queens but, I fear, spangle singular is not nearly enough. A 'dazzle' is perhaps more appropriate, since it extends beyond drag queens' garments to their acts. Drag acts have always dazzled. These days, however, the material that ranges from political satire, homage to Hollywood, homage to Broadway, queer history – all while maintaining spellbinding illusion – collectively and individually dazzles.

A goggle of swimmers

I'm sorry if you are of an aquatic bent. I am principally sorry because my inspiration for this was, of course, a gaggle of geese. A 'goggle' was irresistible. However, as somebody who likes a quotidian plunge, I must say we breast-strokers of the slow lane cannot help but observe the one ubiquitous adornment of the uber-sexy fast lane swimmers: goggles!

A euphemism of estate agents

I have never met an estate agent who is not masterful with euphemism. Sometimes, they are naughtily euphemistic: 'it accommodates a double bed', meaning the room is the exact dimensions of one; and sometimes brilliantly, 'it's well-loved and you get the feeling it has many stories to tell', meaning it needs a lot of TLC. If they do not already have a collective noun, I think this will do nicely.

A harmony of nightingales

Birds, arguably, did best when it comes to collective nouns. Among my favourites are a murder of crows, a crown of kingfishers and a mischief of magpies! But what is the collective noun for our songstresses of Berkeley Square fame, arguably the laryngeal queen of birds? A 'watch'. One can only conclude that the coiner of murders, crowns and mischiefs was on sabbatical by the time they reached N in the ornithological dictionary. Celebrated soloists normally, when together, they are surely a 'harmony'?

How to...
speak like a
movie star

The linguistics of the motion picture industry is as indelible as its films. I fell in love with the 'golden age' of Hollywood when I was knee-high to a grasshopper. I watched my favourite comedy, *Bringing Up Baby*, and my favourite romantic drama, *Brief Encounter*, around seventeen times each before I was twelve! Goodness knows how these films first crossed my path. My parents were not especially enthused by Katharine Hepburn or Celia Johnson. I suppose, when your antennae are up, they are up, and the merest whiff of celluloid magic can start a life-long love affair. I still believe that *Bringing Up Baby* is the perfect comedy, and the quintessence of ...

Screwball

skroo•bawl adjective noun

Screwball is a portmanteau of *screw* and *ball*. Cricketers coined *screwball* in 1866 but it took a long time to fly Stateside and be adopted by the baseball community who started to 'screw' their balls in around 1928. Shortly thereafter it became a metaphor for a person who had all the spin and wild velocity of a screwball. This is why the 1930s screwball comedies orbit the fast-talking nuttiness of their central characters. They are comedies about human screwballs.

Gay

gay adjective

Another reason I am drawn to the screwball comedies of the 1930s may be that they were teeming with gay and bisexual actors. *Bringing Up Baby*'s stars, Cary Grant and Katharine Hepburn, were both dating aviator Howard Hughes at the time of filming, though only Cary joined his mile high club. Cary was still in the grips of his great love story with fellow actor Randolph Scott, and Katharine had rumoured affairs with New York heiress Laura Harding and the reclusive Greta Garbo! These were halcyon days for gays: although not publicly accepted, it was the closest Hollywood ever came to the attitudes of today. And, contrary to popular opinion, this is when the word *gay*, meaning homosexual, entered popular parlance. Look no further than *Bringing Up Baby* (1937) for proof. Katharine Hepburn lures Cary Grant to her aunt's country house with a leopard (you'll just have to watch it). To keep him there, she steals his clothes while he's in the shower. He dons her negligee to cover his modesty. Enter Aunt Elizabeth, who says, 'Why are you wearing those clothes?' Grant's response? 'Because I decided to go gay all of a sudden!'

Box office poison

Another phrase coined in the 1930s that Hollywood movie stars still use is *box office poison*. Katharine Hepburn and her occasional paramour, Greta Garbo, were both on a list of stars with this label who were considered (and here comes another portmanteau) *poisonalities* because of a succession of commercial flops. Garbo was Sweden's most famous export and would sometimes get in a bit of a muddle with these fresh American coinings. On one of her steamy visits to Katharine Hepburn she lamented their both being in the 'poison box'.

Cinema

si•nuh•muh noun

The key word which all these others orbit is, of course, *cinema*. It is a contraction of *cinematograph* from the Greek *kinema*, 'movement' and *graphē*, 'drawing'. Isn't it funny how close 'movement drawings' is to 'moving pictures'? The latter, ultimately, gave us the contraction *movies*. You will probably recognise *kinema* from words like *kinetic*, 'of or relating to movement' and *akinesia*, 'loss of voluntary movement'. Of course, the movement on the screen was everything, since, at the time of these etymological conjurings, we were dealing exclusively with silent films.

Camera

ka•muh•ruh noun

These 'moving pictures' were shot on cameras of enormous heft. *Camera* is also a contraction. It is a contraction of *camera obscura* or 'dark chamber'. Prototype cameras depended on light control. They had to be operated in dark chambers where gradations of light were easy to manage. Today, however, you are more likely to hear camera operators say they are 'chasing the light', meaning that daylight is ebbing and they are determined to get all their shots before it disappears completely!

Shot

shot noun

In the early days of silent movies, film cameras were cranked by hand. So were machine guns. Each *shot*, or second of film, was approximately 24 frames, a bit like a round of bullets. You can see why early filmmakers might liken these vast machines that were designed to be aimed at and focused upon moving targets – and were even similarly operated – to guns.

Tricks

triks noun

I have talked about Hepburn, Grant and their shared lover, but they also shared a platonic love for director George Cukor. Cukor was gay and unique insofar as, although never public about his sexuality (it was illegal and therefore virtually unknown to be in the 1930s), he was totally open in Hollywood circles. Sex work was ubiquitous at this time in Hollywood and Cukor and chums were partial to what were called *tricks*, presumably because the sex workers turned them. Tricks that Cukor was particularly fond of had a habit of popping up in his movies. In fact, one day when flanked by a colleague watching the rushes of his magnificent *Romeo and Juliet*, the colleague asked, 'Is there a reason for that lingering close-up on that very beautiful boy who has no bearing on the plot?' to which Cukor replied, 'Oh yes! A *very good* reason.'

That's a wrap!

Film is full of what are known as linguistic skeuomorphs: in fact, *film* itself is one. A linguistic skeuomorph is what happens when language stubbornly stays in one era while technology has marched on and left it behind. Filming, of course, no longer uses film, but chips. Wrap is, not definitely, but probably, an acronym of 'wind reel and print!' At the end of a film, the director would want the last reel of film wound, printed and subsequently cut.

The cutting room floor

No actor, presenter or even reality television star wants to end up on the cutting room floor: the place the all-powerful edit will send you if a scene lacks sparkle or punch or is deemed superfluous. It is a phrase that is still used but it is another linguistic skeuomorph. After all, there is no film to 'cut'. In fact, the only things you might find on the floors of mostly immaculate editing suites these days are biscuit crumbs.

Jumping the shark

Now this, strictly speaking, is telly rather than movie jargon. We owe the idiom to the brilliant Fonz in *Happy Days*. Ratings, at the shank of this long-running show, were slipping through executive fingers like bath water. They were straining every sinew to devise ways of keeping retinas on goggle boxes. Toward the end of *Happy Days'* colossal run, the Fonz would do such outré things as water-ski, complete with signature leather jacket, and inexplicably jump a shark in the process. It became a metaphor for the desperate acts of artists, and those above them, to salvage the unsalvageable. Like stripping during a floundering eleven o'clock number (*see* page 25) for no conceivable reason.

How to...
wax rhapsodic

Incidentally, this *wax* is a word confined to expressions like the above, and the fattening and slimming of the moon. It simply means to grow. This suits me, since I grow rhapsodic when full of praise, then grow, and then grow a little more. There is never any waning, I'm afraid. That does not mean, however, that an insincere gush has ever proceeded from my larynx. It is more a case of my brain swimming with plaudits and then the boy takes his finger out of the dyke and out they pour.

Ineffably brilliant

Sometimes you see a performance, a work of art or even a garment so exquisite that, temporarily, all words are wrested from you. However, tolerance for the dumbfounded, I have found, is brief. So, I have devised this nifty little phrase for that moment that describes the piece and the awestruck moment contemporaneously. The *brilliant* satisfyingly bounces from the *bly* of *ineffably*, and *ineffably* itself excuses the loss of words. Broken down, the *in* is 'not' and *effabilis* Latin for 'utterable'. If something is unutterably wonderful, saying so with a little bounce and alliteration buys you a good 30 seconds of voiceless wonder.

Plaudits and encomiums

plaw • duht noun,   uhng • kow • mee • uhms noun

The above are two things every writer, performer and artist crave from the critics and seldom receive, at least in an undiluted way. *Plaudit*, etymologically, contains a great deal of that initial, physical reaction to artistic brilliance: *applause*. These lexical sisters share the Latin stem *plaudere*, 'to clap'. An *encomium* is a discerning sort of praise, converted from an equally physical stem. Comos was the Greek God of Festivity. He would follow Dionysus, God of Wine, brandishing a wine-filled goblet to sustain the merriment. Although associated with gay abandon (my favourite kind of abandon), he is also associated with prolonging and sustaining merriment with libations and praise. Because of the gorgeous and unequivocal nature of these words, I often say, when dazzled, 'I have nothing but plaudits and encomiums.'

The devil is in the detail

This phrase is another two-pronged fork for me. It is an

instruction for flattery, since the best compliments are always the result of a keen eye. It is also about the finest elements of art being found in nuance. The phrase itself is, in fact, a stonking great inversion of an old German proverb, *Der liebe Gott steckt im detail*, which means '*God* is in the detail'. The trouble with the original, for me, is that it is one-pronged. It sort of says the mark of God is in the minutiae. Flipping to *devil*, and – I promise I am not just being blasphemous – calls to mind all those effortful phrases like 'I had a devil of a time' or 'It was a devil of a job', which conjure the beautiful pain of detail.

Pulchritudinous

puhl • kruh • choo • duh • nuhs adjective

Not all our rhapsodies are confined to artistic endeavours, I hear you cry. Some, maybe most, are the reserve of individuals. In turn, the lion's share of those are directed towards our lovers. This is where you might like the odd word as lovely as the countenance you are describing. In this group, *pulchritudinous* wears the diadem. It has a music all of its own. It comes from the Latin *pulcher*, meaning 'beautiful'. The secret of the word's beauty is partly its rarity. Her only sibling, I think, is *pulchrify*, meaning to 'beautify'. Words that are alien to our ears, with very few lexical relations, inspire a dance of the grey cells and delight in the ear.

Lepid

leh • puhd adjective

Another word for those you adore. From the Latin *lepidus*, meaning 'charming', the music of obscurity plays again, that you may surprise the ear of lover or friend. You might try, 'You are lepid and lovely,' or, in the wake of a spat, 'You're lucky you're lepid!'

How to...
be brave

It is hard sometimes to countenance all the challenges our age presents. War, climate catastrophe, ever-evolving viruses. If only lexical navigation were all we had to worry about. However, an etymological study of bravery can be a tonic. It speaks to tenacity through time, because the coinings concerning courage are plentiful and inspired. And humanity *is* brave. Not least in our optimism. However existential the threats, we retain a certain faith in our essential goodness, in our ability to ultimately triumph. That is my definition of courage.

Courage

kuh • ruhj noun

Courage is more interesting etymologically than you might think. It is one of those word phenomena where the Latin is cleaved from the Germanic thanks to the influence of French, but both show up in English resulting in approximate synonyms. Courage is, when dissected, behaviour of the strong-hearted, thanks to the Latin *cor*, meaning 'heart', or *hearty* behaviour if you were to favour the Germanic. Both recognise that outer bravery comes from inner determination, normally inspired by love for something we deem more important than fear. Courage is not an etymological solo act: *cordial* describes communication 'of the heart' or, as her Germanic sister would have it, *heartfelt* communication.

> 'Courage cannot see around corners, but goes around them anyway.'
>   – Mignon McLaughlin

One of the many quotable aphorisms of the brilliant Mignon McLaughlin. She was a *Vogue* columnist for decades and was famous for her wit-coated candour. The best kind. Many of her aphorisms, like my favourite, above, concerned bravery. Another of rival popularity is, 'Our strength is often composed of the weakness that we're damned if we're going to show.'

Brave new world

Miranda, in Shakespeare's *The Tempest*, lives most of her life marooned on a Mediterranean island. Her father, Prospero, is disillusioned with the old world from whence they came. When erstwhile enemies from that world are shipwrecked on their island, however, Miranda is captivated, declaring, 'Oh brave new world, that has such people in't.' This use of brave is more akin to its siblings *bravo* and *bravura*, meaning 'bold'. But we have since reinterpreted this famous line. Today, it tends to mean a world one has to be brave to meet, one full of terrible things. It is an ironic take on Miranda's original utterance.

Gird your loins

Gird your loins rests very neatly under our substantial skeuomorph parasol. It is an archaic version of *roll up your sleeves* to prepare for strenuous activity. The girdle was, for biblical fashionistas, a substantial belt, and loins, in this case, a contraction of loin cloths or cloths that hung about your loins. For physical exertion in these pre-joggers days, one would hitch these loins into one's girdle, hence gird*ing* them. And lo! You are ready for any doughty pursuit.

Brace yourself

We probably have the Normans to thank for this one. It is that very physical feeling of the erect preparedness one feels when one locks one's arms, or *bras* if you are French. *Bras* pops up in all sorts of places: *Bra*, short for *brassière*, a supportive garment using straps above and below the arms and *embrace*, where one is enveloped in another's arms.

Courage is the father of success

This old Nigerian proverb is more pertinent today than when it was coined. Success can only be achieved with bold, courageous policy-makers to mitigate the problems that make our planet ache and groan. Part of the bravery lies in the originality required. The ideas will have to be in an entirely new cast to tackle our unprecedented problems.

Intrepid

in • treh • puhd *adjective*

I like this synonym for 'fearless' more than any other because it conveys a sense of unphased stoicism. The *in* means 'not' and, at its core, is the Latin *trepidus*, meaning 'alarmed'. That is the most successful kind of fearlessness in my experience: the variety where a cool mind triumphs over alarming surroundings; where clarity wins over panic.

Impavid

im • pah • vuhd *adjective*

True, 'intrepid' is hard to top etymologically but, if you want a literal synonym for fearless that is more aurally satisfying, look no further. *Impavid*, from the Latin *im*, meaning 'not' and *pavidus*, meaning 'fearful', is waiting in the wings, eager to dance on the tip of your tongue. Apologies for mixed metaphors although, I confess, I am impavid about the occasional metaphor melange.

Stoicism

stow • uh • si • zm *noun*

Would you believe *stoicism* is *cynicism's* baby? Neither word meant to their original Ancient Greek founders what they mean today. The Cynics' belief was that happiness was achieved by a celebration of the natural and rejection of social constructs. They did not believe in law, society or possessions. In fact, Diogenes, father of Cynicism, once smashed his only cup because he saw a sproglet drinking water using his hands and was outraged by his own seduction by societal norms (even cup-buying was conformist to a true Cynic). The Stoics were reverential about the Cynics, after all they were an offshoot of their branch of philosophy. Stoics, however, believed that nothing could be *more* natural for humanity than to create civilisation; that our desire to respect our fellow man was supported by society and it should be lovingly maintained. They felt that even if you erased the memory of civilisation and started all over again, humanity would create it anyway. The idea of *cynicism*, as we know it today, must come from the many societal things the Cynics rejected and were sceptical about, as opposed to the many things they were for. The modern notion of *stoicism* must come from the Stoics' steadfast defence of society's constructs.

Pluck

pluhk noun verb

We admire plucky people. The word is invariably used fondly. But have you ever pondered the etymology of 'pluck'? In the 1600s, *pluck* was all that you would 'pluck' from the bodies of farm animals before they were sold as food. The pluck, therefore, included the heart and guts. We are all familiar with having guts and being gutsy as descriptions of bravery, and the etymology of *courage* tells us how big a role the heart plays. The pluck that was plucked contained all the etymological ingredients of bravery. I do hope your pluck is never plucked.

How to...
describe what
you do (and
how you are
remunerated)

I am often asked, if I were not a performer/television floozy, what would I be? The answer: I haven't the foggiest idea. I have no discernible skillset outside that world and even my extracurricular pastimes are theatre-centric. Mercifully, there is at least a word for my rather blinkered condition ...

Fachidiot

fack • i • dee • uht noun

This German word really does describe me. Somebody whose skill set is so exclusively funnelled into their chosen vocation, or *fach*, 'subject', that they are an 'idiot' where anything else is concerned. It is a kind of narrowness of thought. The word implies the idiocy is a symptom of the fachidiot's total preoccupation with their elected field. Now for a word or two on remuneration ...

Kuidaore

kwee • doray verb

This is really the notion of 'champagne on a cider budget', or whatever that elusive expression is. It means, literally, 'to eat yourself into ruin'. *Kui* is Japanese for 'eating' and *daoreru*, 'to be ruined'. That well-known phenomenon of one's tastes not matching one's bank balance!

Jugaad

juhg • ahd verb

Jugaad is a Hindi word that approximately means to 'make do and mend'. To jugaad is to cleverly find the best interim solution when funds are tight. My dad used to describe my erstwhile theatrical existence as 'living off the smell of an oily rag'. It is a little bit that.

Sometimes people find themselves pining for those oily rag days. It is a sentiment that finds its way into many songs and poems. Neil Sedaka's plaintive 'The Hungry Years' juxtaposes romantic music with stark lyrics, like this lyrical French phrase, *Nostalgie de la boue*.

This phrase translates as 'nostalgia for the mud'. It is the Tom and Barbara feeling in *The Good Life*. After all Tom's high-flying success in the world of business he finds himself longing for the ultimate primitive existence. Living simply, humbly and, in their case literally from *la boue*, to go the whole hog and become self-sufficient.

Here is a word for lexicographers and anarchists alike …

Radical

ra • duh • kl adjective noun

Radic is the Latin root meaning 'root'. We cannot have a book of roots without looking at the root-root now, can we? *Radish* is of course an obvious offspring. It means, simply, 'root', which, after all, is all a radish is. *Eradicating* is a 'rooting out'. A *radical* is a less obvious relative. It is a person who 'challenges the roots'. One who believes that real change comes from pulling the perceived weeds out by the root. After all, as we green-fingered types know all too well, snipping the offenders will never suffice!

Salary

sa • luh • ree noun

Sal is the Latin root meaning 'salt'. It is liberally sprinkled into *saline*, meaning 'salty'. It's a great big stretch to get from here to one's wages! Though perhaps not, for the Romans. Their salary was their 'salt money', so the word is a wonderful precursor to phrases like 'bread-winner' and 'bringing home the bacon'. Dosh equals grub!

Iniquity

ih • ni • kwuh • tee noun

Aequus is the Latin root meaning 'equal'. It is a generous root in its dissemination throughout our language: *equable* is equal tempered, in other words possessing emotional equilibrium.

Equanimity is equal (or balanced) mindedness, and *equivalent* is having equal value. *Iniquity*, however, refers to immoral or naughty behaviour. How did this warped branch proceed from this otherwise consistent, girthy trunk? In fact, the definition we have today comes via observers of 'unequalness'. Therein lies sin. If you think of the famed Victorian 'dens of iniquity', this was always true. There, the vices were necessitated by poverty and enjoyed by the rich; the wealthy lord and the penurious sex worker, for example. Hence the dens of 'unequalness' or iniquity became the dens of transgression or ... iniquity.

Aspiration

ah • spuh • ray • shn *noun*

Spirare is the Latin root meaning 'to breathe'. *Respiration*, therefore, is a 'breathing back', describing the act of breathing. Now that we have inhaled, let's spirit towards the *spirit* which undams the rest of the tributaries. The spirit is 'the breath', in other words 'the life' inside us. With that in mind, when we talk *aspiration*, it is that which you 'breathe towards', in other words, the aim of one's directed spirit. Similarly, *conspire* is 'breathe together' or 'spirits together' in a scheme. Might we argue that Pavarotti, at 32 bars a note, was the most spirited man who ever lived?

How to...
talk about
money
(if you must)

This is many people's least favourite topic but, unlike other unpopular talking points, it must be discussed periodically. Fiscal conversations happen with alarming regularity and, even with fiscal professionals, they can be embarrassing. As with all tricky topics, however, words can mitigate, mask and even excuse the speaker through their employment. Euphemism and well-chosen synonyms demonstrate the speaker's desire to be as delicate as possible.

Chrometophobia

krow • muh • tuh • fow • bee • uh noun

Most of us have a phobia of discussing money but is there a phobia of money itself? *Chrometophobia* is just that. From the Greek *chrimata*, meaning 'money' and *phobia*, it is a rare condition characterised by extreme fear of spending money. We talk a about frugality and thrift in quite casual terms, but chrometophobia takes these to dizzying heights. Disinclination to spend becomes terror.

Brassic

brae • suhk adjective

One might be more susceptible to chrometophobia if one has endured prolonged periods of being *brassic*. *Brassic*'s roots lie in cockney rhyming slang. It is a contraction of the phrase *boracic lint* which rhymes with 'skint'. To further confine the rhyming slang to the tribe it was intended for, the rhyming element would be lopped off so that, only through knowing the erstwhile rhyme, could one decode. Take 'bottle of *pig's*', only decipherable if you know *pig's* is short for *pig's ear* which rhymes with *beer*. Thus, *boracic* became the post-trim rhyming slang for skint, and resulted in the subsequent mini-mangling, *brassic*.

Munificent

myoo • ni • fuh • snt adjective

The polar opposite of a chrometophobe might be a *munificent* person. It is a synonym for *generous*, but I find the etymology of generosity vexing. In Latin, *generosus* is 'of noble birth', so there is a feudal implication here: the overflowing bounty of the rich. Not altogether lovely. Munificence, on the other hand, is. It comes from the Latin *munus*, meaning 'gift'. It is a gift-giving as opposed to excess-donating. Munificence has enormous heart.

Flush

fluhsh noun verb

Flush is a word with about fifty meanings attached to it. One of these is to be 'in the money'. It may connect to another of flush's many meanings; to be *flush* with something is to physically meet it. For river water to be flush with its banks, the river would have to be full. This notion extended to coins in a coffer being flush with its top.

Line the coffers

Another skeuomorph that has, I am delighted to say, stayed with us. Curiously, we might easily have said something quite spooky when collecting funds. We might, etymologically speaking, have been lining our coffins. *Coffin* and *coffer* are close sisters, because they are both transmutations of the Latin *cophinus*, meaning 'basket'. Had these transmutations reversed, we would be filling our coffins with funds and our coffers with corpses.

Pocketbook

po • kuht buk noun

This word is terribly useful as a fiscal euphemism. It was originally a pocket-sized binding containing financial papers, bills and bumf. It became a purse *c.* 1816 and subsequently gave birth to a slew of euphemisms, particularly in the States: *O ye of swollen pocketbook, slender pocketbook, hit me in the pocketbook* and *in pocketbook pursuit.*

How to... describe just how far you would like to go, how much you want and when

Distances. Size. Quantity. They inspire both the hyperbolic and the forensically accurate. For the former, some of the entries in this chapter have become linguistic skeuomorphs that are automatically hyperbolic when compared to today's incredibly precise measuring tools. For the latter, in lieu of modern measuring tools, pinpoint accuracy was conveyed by describing the tiniest conceivable margins. Even with recognised units, however, as we shall see with *miles*, measurements can be as stretchy as knicker elastic.

Block

blok noun

The *block* is sometimes more formally referred to as the Manhattan Metric. Because New York is famously grid-like, it can roughly be divided into rectangles of 80 274 m / 262 × 899 ft. The short side (80 m / 262 ft) of the rectangle is the street-to-street measurement, so it is a wonderfully economic way of conveying distance to a friend. This is perhaps the only word in this book that is untranslatable due simply to distinctive municipal design.

A hair's breadth

This phrase was probably popularised by our old friend from the world of insults, William Shakespeare. I adore it because one is hard pushed to think of any breadth or 'width' narrower than that of a hair. As the narrowest imaginable margin, it's a tremendous phrase for jeopardy: one can win, lose, escape, survive, all by a hair's breadth. Let's see it employed by the ultimate dramatist ...

> 'Wherein I spake of most disastrous chances,
> Of moving accidents by flood and field,
> Of hair-breadth 'scapes i' th'imminent
> deadly breach.'
> — William Shakespeare, *Othello*

And speaking of narrow margins ...

By a canvas

You may have heard, and been foxed, by this curious expression. You may know that it means 'by a very small margin' but be puzzled as to why. It comes from world boat racing where the front of the boat, to allow sea water to easily trickle off, was covered in canvas. In extremely tight races it may come down to nudging ahead with no more than a canvas-sheathed bow.

The nautical world has given popular parlance many measurements. The one most employed by my family indicates that we have reached quafftide ...

The sun is over the yard arm

On old ships, when one might be at sea for a very long time, one needed a way of telling the time. The yard arm served as rudimentary nautical sundial. The sun was, of course, directly over the yard arm at midday. Apparently, in the world of the early sailor, noon was a suitable time for a first libation. It is a small wonder, then, that inebriation and seamen were inextricably linked in sea shanties like 'What Shall We Do with the Drunken Sailor?' I hasten to add (although my dad is a sailor) that we take the expression less literally in our family. Over our spectral yard arm the sun hovers at around seven o'clock. Six, if it has been an extremely taxing day.

Poronkusema

poron • kyoo • see • mah noun

Of course, many early measurements were experiential: the sun signalling quafftide on a boat, tiny margins conveyed by the narrowest part of one's own anatomy, etc. Best of all, for the Finns, was the distance travelled before your reindeer needed to spend a penny. If you are interested, that is about 7.6 km / 4.7 miles. A *poronkusema* is that between-bathroom-breaks measurement and, once upon a time, an extremely useful one. It is nice to know that reindeer are not only dazzlingly beautiful, but staggeringly regular.

Now for a little unit and measurement etymology. After all, the ingredients in the words we know are often as surprising as the definitions of the ones we do not ...

Ingredient

uhng•gree•dee•uhnt noun

Gradus is the Latin root meaning 'to step'. It is a short 'step', therefore, to *grades*, the 'steps' on a metaphorical path, *gradual*, 'step by step' and *gradient*, referring to the depth of step required. But how does our *ingredient* hop into this curious recipe? I have almost said it! It is a substance or thing that 'steps into' the mixture. Therefore, any ingredient that happens to have a 'kick' to it, is spot on.

Mile

mile noun

Mille is the Latin root meaning 1,000. A *millenium* is a thousand years, a *million* a thousand thousands, a *millimetre* a thousandth of a metre, etc. But a *mile* is not a thousand anything! After all, there are 1,760 yards in a mile. Confusingly, the mile has been considerably augmented since it was coined! Originally it was the sum of 1,000 Roman paces. If reverted, marathon runners would be heaving a combined sigh of relief, big enough to generate a large zephyr!

November

now•vem•buh noun

Novem is the Latin root meaning 'nine'. How comfortably, therefore, this root finds itself in *nonagenarian,* a person in their nineties! But what twit would name the eleventh month of the year the ninth? A Roman. And please don't take offence if you are a Roman spectre hovering over these pages. I now know that in your calendar – which began in March – November really *was* the ninth month!

doo•zee *noun*

An invaluable North American word
because it is without judgment.
A doozy is that which ranks top,
whether good or bad: you could
have a doozy of a fight or a doozy
of wedding.

Ides of March

Ides is an ancient Latin word meaning 'to divide'. The division in question refers to the lunar cycle, which would recommence roughly in the middle of each Roman calendar month. There was a notion, among the superstitious, that one's fortunes could change at this point, but in March it had less to do with the moon and more to do with the coffers. You may have heard about the *Ides of March* exclusively in the context of something to 'beware' of. This was debt collectors' moment to shine in the fiscal year. They held no prisoners and, for many, the Ides of March were not a happy time.

Halfly

haaf·lee adjective adverb noun

Even though language has been more than generous to us, there are times when you think 'here's a logical progression', or 'if there's this, why not *that*', and there is no answer. I always say, if in doubt, coin. Fiscally, contractually, or even because of natural patterns, we sometimes cut our year in four. We call those four chunks of time *quarterly* periods. But when we are describing corresponding patterns that take place in only the first and second halves of the year, we call them *bi-annual*. If we have *quarterly* events, surely, we can have *halfly* ones? Apart from anything else, it is such a dear little word.

Eftsoons

eft·soons adverb

This Old English word is sadly obsolete. It means very soon afterwards, since *eft* is 'again' and soon is 'early'. So, this *afterwards* is at the earliest opportunity. Let's go to the ballet tonight and have a coup of champagne eftsoons, meaning as soon as the curtain falls. My hope is, once this book hits the shelves, *eftsoons* returns eftsoons!

Universal

yoo • nuh • vuh • sl adjective noun

Unus is the Latin root meaning 'one'. The root is quite logically found in *unique* as, of course, the 'only one' of its kind and *unit*, which is 'one thing'. But doesn't *universal*, conversely, seem vast, sprawling, widespread? It is! But in its *oneness*. The oneness has become ubiquitous when something becomes universal. One is not the loneliest number after all.

The nth degree

This is a measurement of the unmeasurable. In algebra, since the eighteenth century, n represented the unquantifiable number and, therefore, to *the nth degree* has been part of mathematical discourse for 300 years. It bounced from textbooks into popular usage about 100 years later. I use it to the nth degree.

Analysis

uh • na • luh • suhs noun

Lyein is the Greek root meaning 'loosen'. All those lovely 'lyses' words are loosenings of chemical structures via whatever their prefix happens to be. So *hydrolysis* uses water to loosen a chemical structure and *electrolysis* uses electricity. But what about *analysis*? Surely this is the reverse? To me the word conjures an examination with a fine-toothed comb. Ah! But that fine-toothed comb is loosening the structure or elements to examine or analyse its constituent parts. Isn't it dazzling how – with a little analysis – a connection that seems remote at best, reveals itself to be astonishingly close?

Vague

vayg *adjective*

Vagus is the Latin root meaning 'wandering'. It wanders into *vagrants* and *vagabonds*, both meaning 'wandering people' because they are without a permanent home. But *vague*? What has the ill-defined and delineated to do with wandering? It is because the vague wanders over lines of definition. Like a metaphoric vagrant, what is vague in thought or expression is never stationary, for if it stopped wandering it would be able to be defined.

Fuck off

I am not being rude. It is simply that, bizarrely and brilliantly, *fuck off* has become a measurement of sorts. It simply conveys that something is gargantuan. You will hear people talk about climbing a 'fuck-off mountain' or demolishing a 'fuck-off breakfast' and they don't mean that the mountain or the breakfast disappeared but that it was simply enormous. I love the totally inexplicable nature of this. I like to embrace the surreal and *fuck off* as a size-denoter really fits the bill.

TIDSOPTIMISM

tid • sop • tuh • mis • uhm *noun*

The state of cheerful faith in the
elasticity of time, resulting in
cramming too much into a day.

How to... sashay with sartorial elegance

In the Introduction I said that the words we select, the words we omit and the words we favour create the most intimate portrait of us. The other contenders in self-portraiture, however, are strong. They are our politics, our actions, our tastes and our wardrobe. What we wear says so much that it has generated an entire lexicon of its own and can elicit some fairly fabulous phrases.

My coloury hat

To my sister's chagrin, Artie, for the first four years of his life had no interest in clothes whatsoever. When they moved to Didsbury I was always struck by the high street, prettily dotted with elegant boutiques. We met at a local pub, had a super lunch and a post-prandial stroll along the high street, Artie sitting proudly atop my shoulders. We got caught in the window's sway of one of these lovely boutiques. It was then that Artie offered his first ever sartorial opinion. Spying a deliciously outré, rainbow-striped woollen bobble hat, he said, 'Uncle Tom, I *love* that coloury hat!' I do not know which I found more exciting: Artie's exquisite choice or the coining of the word 'coloury'. So overwhelmed with delight was I, that I offered Artie the coloury hat. He wears it to this day.

Sartorial wizardry

This is a phrase of my own invention (though I have no doubt it has been said before). Sometimes, I think the assembly of a particularly arresting outfit is tantamount to sorcery. If I feel it, I must also say it. Compliments are no good dancing on one's frontal lobe. They must always be uttered.

Clobber

klo•buh noun verb

Clobber, in Victorian times, was a handy leather sealant which meant expensive shoes did not have to be replaced or sent to the cobbler (and yes, I suspect there may be a connection between the two words, since one became a home cobbler with clobber). When smart events took place, for those who could not afford a new ensemble for every function, one might clobber up with sealed shoes and patched garments to achieve sartorial wizardry. Eventually the word 'clobber' became the result of these efforts, and the verb became obsolete.

Chic en noir

sheek ong nuh • waa noun

You can, of course, substitute *noir* for any colour in which somebody happens to look chic. I wear a lot of black because it is so flattering. It becomes every countenance. *Chic* may be my favourite French word. The etymology is uncertain, but a strong contender is the French *chicanerie*, meaning 'trickery'. We are back to sartorial wizardry. If this etymology is correct, the notion is that chicness is achieved by a vestiary chicanery.

Ensemble

on • som • bl noun

Ensemble comes from the Latin *simul*, meaning 'at the same time'. It is the same *simul* we see in *simultaneous*. In music, an ensemble will play simultaneously. Similarly, in the theatre, the ensemble will always appear on stage simultaneously. In fashion terms, it is a collection of garments worn simultaneously. It refers to the whole effect. 'I love your ensemble' acknowledges the care taken in the composition of the whole look. The *ensemble* is as much about the art of assembly – perhaps the greatest sartorial art – as it is about each individual element.

Illusion is the first of all pleasures

One person who adored the chicanery of illusion was Oscar Wilde. The care applied to the knot of his tie, the tilt of his hat, the fall of his cape was omnipresent. In fact, this line originally looked like this: *L'illusion est le premier plaisir*, from the equally elegant Voltaire in his poem *La Pucelle d'Orléans* (The Maid of Orleans).

Cock up your beaver

I have not taken a break from fashion to be very rude indeed. Oh no! The above, I assure you, is all about fashion. Oscar Wilde reminded me of it since his beaver was always cocked. Robert Burns, in his poem of the same name, instructs 'Cock up your beaver, and cock it fu' sprush!' meaning fully turn up the brim of your hat! Every Scot would have understood this instruction. Beaver felt hats were brimmed, and both warm and stylish. Cock, meaning lift, is something we have retained in a handful of phrases such as *cock your head* – meaning lift it – and *cock up*, meaning something has been lifted upside down and is, therefore, a helluva mess.

Threads

thredz noun

We think of *lit threads*, meaning 'uber-chic garments', as a very contemporary phrase. Actually, it dates back to 1926 and the height of the Jazz Age in America. This age was as generous to idiom as it was to music. And, appropriately enough, the idioms had music inbuilt: 'You look like *the bees knees*,' or this, sadly confined to the Jazz Age, 'You are *the elephant's ears*.'

Piccadilly

pi • kuh • di •lee noun

Here is a vestiary word that has left more of a mark on maps than fashion. If you lived in London, Manchester or New York – in the days of the legendary Hotel Piccadilly, on 45th Street, west of Broadway – *piccadilly* was a very familiar word. But it has nothing to do with big streets or grand edifices. It has to do with lace. Roger Baker was the Vivienne Westwood of his day and, in the seventeenth century you couldn't out-chic his lace collars, known as *piccadills*. Piccadilly, in London and in Manchester, were the epicentres of the lace trade and the beloved *piccadills*, which, as seventeenth-century portraiture attests, were ubiquitous. Their popularity lined local coffers which, in turn, made Piccadillys very fashionable districts. Ultimately, this meant that they became more famous for their hotels and eateries than for their lace production. By the time the Hotel Picadilly was christened in New York in 1928, I suspect nobody knew about the lost *piccadill*, only about that vast street in London, home to the Ritz since 1906, Fortum & Mason and a slew of other 'must-go's' for the affluent American abroad.

Puttin' on the Ritz

The jewel in Piccadilly's diadem, the Ritz is unique in the hotel world in lending her name to fashion. When hotelier César Ritz open his original eponymous hotel in Paris in 1898, he created a phenomenon. Before the gram (Instagram), before Twitter, everyone seemed to have heard about this magical place. Eight years later, the doors of the Paris Ritz's younger sister opened to Londoners. By 1930, so synonymous was the Ritz with style and glamour, Irving Berlin, legendary showtune pensmith, coined the phrase, 'Puttin' on the Ritz', in his song of the same name. It was a euphemism for scaling sartorial heights. In fact, Harry Richman, in the 1930 film *Puttin' On The Ritz* was decked out in top hat and tails in just the same way Fred Astaire was when he put the song on celluloid for a second time in the hugely successful *Blue Skies*, in 1946. These images were disseminated worldwide, and even for those who had never heard of the Ritz, the notion of puttin' it on or, subsequently, looking ritzy, were universally understood.

On fleek

This term is not exclusively, but mostly, confined to the fashion world. *Fleek*, according to the *Urban Dictionary*, was coined back in 2003 and meant 'smooth, nice, sweet'. Now, I am no great authority on urban lexicon, but I don't think fleek really caught on as a solo act. *On fleek*, however, is a different story. It so perfectly encapsulates the chic and the modern that (don't curdle, kids) I have found myself using it on occasion.

Box-fresh creps

There is a curious gossamer thread that links young athletes delighting in their *box-fresh creps* (trainers so new they still smell of the box) and Ancient Greek athletes in their *krepis*, which were robust woven-soled, many-strapped sandals perfect for athletes – if you ignore the perils of a javelin and an open toe. Mind you, this was a vast improvement on the barefoot Olympians that preceded them. There is a strong possibility, too, given the common athletic purpose of the *krepis* and the crep, that they both (in their respective times) double up as uber-chic accessories, that the former lives in the latter, etymologically speaking.

Birthday suit

When all is said and done, however cool the threads, however chic the clobber, my favourite suit will always be my *birthday suit*. I sleep in it nightly, nothing on. Well, except for Radio 4, that is. This notion of the 'suit' you were born in is, in fact, plus âgé. The German *mutternackt* is a very old word meaning 'mother naked', as naked as one's first stitchless appearance. It is a baby step, if you'll pardon the almost unpardonable pun, to the suit of the day of your birth. It is, undoutedly, everybody's loveliest outfit.

How to... navigate the many metaphors of sex

Sex. Where to begin? I'm going to buck the trend set by the world's most famous nun and not 'start at the very beginning', after all, given her calling, her advice might be malapropos here. Instead, I'm going to fast-forward to (arguably) the best bit: the orgasm. The first imported orgasm-appellation listed here may, at first glance, seem rather macabre ...

Petite mort

puh • teet maw noun

This divinely dark French term literally translates as 'little death'. I can understand this. Try and remember the orgasms that really penetrate the upper echelons (for luckier readers, that memory may be fresher than it is for your unfortunate author): your mind leaves your body, your heart seems to stop beating and everything, for just one moment, becomes metaphysical. This instant of bliss is barely a living state. The French would go even further and say it is the opposite: it is a glimpse of death.

Gao chao

gau chau noun

Mandarin gives us *gao chao* or 'high tide' for orgasm. Every cell is at high tide when on the brink of orgasm. Sexual organs are loaded with juices that they are about to expel and blood cells visit en mass, creating a high tide that laps the shores of frenzied nerve endings.

Scopare

skoh • pah • ray verb

One must head to Italy for what I consider to be the loveliest euphemism for lovemaking. *Scopare* actually means 'to sweep'. If you slow down any kind of sweeping action, you will find it somewhat reminiscent of sex. Think about it for a moment: you descend, you often make some kind of contact, then you swoop up again with a wonderful flourish to finish. And repeat.

Frottage

frot • aazh noun

Frottage is that lovely portion of lovemaking where, at the risk of sounding unromantic, your bodies explore the sexiness of friction. The almost static-electric thing of rubbing various bits together as protrusion finds nook and bulge finds cranny. Etymologically, again, we have our French cousins to thank for this glorious word, since *frotter* is French for 'to rub'.

Do you smoke after sex?

Post-coital-cigarette-puffing is an image indelibly seared on the mind's eye thanks to the movies. The greatest sex wit of the last century was surely the incomparable Mae West. Although much quoted, you may not know this line – my personal favourite – since it is merely anecdotal. John Gielgud was probing her about her post-coital customs one day, and asked, 'Do you smoke after sex, Mae?' She replied, 'I don't know ...', offered a cursory glance to her nether regions and finished with '... I never checked.'

Testicle

teh • stuh • kl   noun

Testis is the Latin root meaning 'witness'. It stands to reason, therefore, that most of its tributaries flow logically from this root: to *attest* is to bear witness, *testimony* is one's witness statement and to *testify* is to offer that statement. So, what, you may legitimately ask, have bollocks got to do with all of this? Well, the link is tenuous, to be sure, but *testicles* are 'little witnesses' to semen secretion and their little bollock retinas are fixed upon the act of ejaculation to ensure all runs smoothly.

Gonorrhoea

go • nuh • ree • uh   noun

Rhoia is the Greek root meaning 'a flow'. This root flows easily, if somewhat pungently, into *diarrhoea*, which means 'a flowing through' ... of poo. As we know, poo ought not really to flow, so in this subtle nod to consistency, we have skirted the yuckiness. But gonorrhoea? 'Link the venereal disease to its root!' I hear you cry. Very well then. It means 'a flowing of seed' because physicians once believed that the discharge that sometimes accompanies it was a kind of – for want of a superior phrase – funky spunk.

Bukkake

boo • kaa • kee *verb*

From the Japanese, *bukkake* is the 'act of splashing'. Because of the 'splash' of sauce, it is the name for a well-loved, well-saturated noodle dish. But this is not the reason *bukkake* is indelibly seared on my mental retina. I learned this word when I was part of a company of actors mounting the Christmas pantomime *Sleeping Beauty*. My opening scene was the great christening-crashing, spell-casting scene that seals the baby's fate. The cradle faced upstage, and I would wield my wand and thrust it in at the recumbent doll on my last, venomous line. The prince in our company was divine, naughty and the only corpser (*see* corpsing in *How to speak like a thespian*, page 23) worse than I. We are chums to this day. I was very green in those days, and our impish prince took it upon himself to daily augment the racier portion of my vocabulary. One day he taught me the word *bukkake*. I cannot remember whether he employed the Japanese 'act of splashing' etymology, but he did inform me that it described a contemporaneous splashing that concludes a sex act. This grand finale centres around the person who first inspired the splash. In case I forgot my new word, my benevolent prince would install a printout as an aide-memoire in the cradle, where the recumbent babe should have been. My last line of Latin vitriol would have to struggle out, no matter what my dilated pupils were ingesting.

How to... describe each chapter of a love affair

For those of you who know me solely as the author of this book, you will not know that I am better known as the ear/shoulder/bosom on the E4 dating programme *Celebs Go Dating*. I am also the 'dating guru' on Capital FM radio. As such, I felt I would be cheating anyone who came to this book via those channels if I did not take a walk through the lexical forest of relationships. But before we get lost in the sprawling woodlands of love, before your shoe has even left its first imprint, we begin with a twinkle ...

Tiam

tee • ahm noun verb

Imagine you are strolling on one of the beautiful beaches of the Iranian island of Kish, and coming the other way is a breathtaking local who seems to be twinkling at you. Iranians would refer to that first love-twinkle as a *tiam*. Singular insofar as it is the commencement twinkle. The beginning.

Green gowning

A little after tiam has occurred, and you have relocated from beaches to fields, you might embark on a bit of *green gowning*. This is a Georgian, bucolic euphemism, where young lovers may trip through fields to find a spot for their first amorous jostle. The vigour of this lovemaking and the lushness of the grass would, of course, have an impact on the garments you were in too much of a hurry to take off, so one's gown is apt to turn green!

Osculation

os • kyoo • lay • shn noun

One key feature, I hope, of your first green gowning will be liberal *osculation*. This beautiful synonym for kissing has as delicious an etymological history as it has a sexy present. *Osculum* is the Latin for 'little mouth', and refers to the pout we make to make ourselves labially (in the lip sense) available to our fellow osculator. Osculation gives us other useful words that use kissing metaphorically, like *osculant*. If you talk about, say, France and her osculant countries, you would be talking about her neighbours such as Switzerland, Germany and Italy, because they are 'kissing' her border.

A kiss is a lovely trick designed by nature to stop speech when words become superfluous.

While we are on osculation, I have to include my favourite utterance on the subject. It proceeded from the osculum of actor, Ingrid Bergman. I think we have all had this moment at least once in our lives. Discourse peters, not because it refuses to come, but because suddenly the form of the mouth conveying ideas to you begins to supersede the ideas in importance. There is a tacit understanding that the silence is an overture and, as it swells, you find your mouths meeting. It is indeed a lovely trick. Bergman had a complex relationship with kissing. She was a passionate person, but her innate ardour had to be curbed on the silver screen. Hollywood had strict rules about kissing and sex in the 1940s. Even if a married couple was sitting on a bed, one person had to keep a foot on the floor. Kisses were even more taboo. They could not exceed three seconds. How, then, did Ingrid Bergman and Cary Grant manage a two-minute, forty-second kissing scene in Alfred Hitchcock's 1946 film *Notorious*? Answer: I personally counted 19 individual kisses, many barely a second long. There are nearly as many osculums that do not quite meet but are purred through. It is genuinely steamy.

Ti voglio bene

tee vol•yo beh•neh noun

While tiam, osculation and green gowning are lovely, eventually one wants to graduate to loving someone 'warts and all'. However, as romantic expressions go, 'warts and all' does not really cut the mustard. Infinitely lovelier is the Italian *ti voglio bene*, which literally translates, 'I want you well'. This is the sustaining love, the love that 'loves well' because it encompasses the whole person. It is loving enhanced by an intimate knowledge of one's paramour.

TRINOCTIAL

TRINOCTIAL

TRINOCTIAL

trai•nok•ti•al *noun*

A simple way of describing a
long weekend – especially a
getaway – where 'three nights'
is the typical duration.

Paramour

pa • ruh • muor noun

Literally, 'through love'. In the days of impenetrable class systems in France, your matches may be made with position and money in mind. The extramarital lovers that both sexes enjoyed were known as paramours or 'through-loves', since they were not arranged, but organic love matches, often shrouded in secrecy. The spouses might well have been called *parargents*, therefore. Of course, over time, these society matches melted away, but paramours remained. Its revised definition is far less euphemistic and much closer to 'lover'. But sometimes paramours stop returning your feelings and your calls, resulting in ...

La douleur exquise

lah doo • luh uhs • skweez noun

Which translates from the French as 'the exquisite pain'. There is a lexical French fashion for juxtaposing extremes. We have often heard that love is the closest relative of hate. We know from petit mort that, arguably, the greatest natural ecstasy in life is as close as we get to glimpsing death. And the harpoon-like pang of unrequited love is somehow beautiful and exquisite. Of course, it is the inspiration of many Chansons Françaises and a quarter of all English language love songs.

Passion

pa • shn noun

The marriage of opposites is most present in the word *passion*. From *pati*, you may be surprised to learn, the Latin root meaning 'to suffer'. It gives us words like *patience*, 'a silent suffering' and *compassion*, 'to suffer with'. *Passion* is the purest transmutation of the Latin root. Romantic passion is connected to the intensity of feeling connected with suffering. Love makes one's being suffer. It is an exquisite pain that the body endures.

Betrothed

buh • trowthd noun

Sometimes the etymology of a word absolutely curdles you and sometimes it inspires. The *troth* in *betrothed* is the Old English 'truth'. To betroth is, etymologically speaking, to offer your 'truth' or 'solemn pledge' to your partner. It gives the act of betrothal tremendous gravity and significance.

For better or worse – oh dear, Percival Pun is back – our relationship-centric language bears the attitudes of its coiners. As a result, we see the strange bedfellows of male chauvinism and romance forever flanking each other ...

Matrimony

ma • truh • muh • nee noun

Mater is the Latin root meaning 'mother'. Fittingly, it is a matriarch root to *maternity*, motherhood and *maternal*, mother-like. But what about this curious off-shoot, *matrimony*, meaning marriage? It is what we now call a linguistic skeuomorph: where time has marched on, but language is (sometimes uncomfortably) clasping to a bygone era. The word was coined in the days when marriage was regarded as a direct conduit to 'mother-status'. That, etymologically, is alas all that matrimony means. Sometimes, dear reader, etymology is an unsavoury mistress. Should matrimony live up to its itchy etymology, you would have an ...

Infant

in • fnt noun

Infans is the Latin root meaning 'not speaking'. This marches silently into *infantry*, the foot soldiers of junior rank who would not speak orders. *Infant* was once much more specific than our current understanding. It referred exclusively to pre-verbal children. I, therefore, in this book of words, would like to protest. Anybody who is au fait with pre-verbal infants will know that they tend to be vociferous, and never short on speech. It is just that in the main it is not quite discernible language yet. But I cavil. I should not get too hung up on semantics; after all, it is not like I'm penning a book on the subject.

Adore

uh • daw verb

Orare is the Latin root meaning 'to speak'. The word *oracle* means a conduit for God's speech. *Oratory* is, equally satisfactorily, the act of 'speech making'. *Adore* is curiously rogue here. But what if adoration were originally exclusively spoken? And behold! Our answer! The word was inextricably connected to praise of the oral variety. These days, mercifully, one may be physical in one's adoration, too.

How to...
be naughty
but nice

This, evidently, is a two-pronged fork. One prong is naughty, coated in niceness; the other, nice coated in naughtiness. The coating varies in thickness, but even a patina can mitigate the effect of the prong it covers. While both tines – I felt I had rather overused prong – are useful in daily discourse, both benefit from their mitigating outer layer.

Boner!

bow • nuh *noun*

As the greatest lover of swearing I know, my mother's repertoire is remarkably small and her delight in discovering new naughty words, palpable. The best example of this was her discovery of the word *boner*. If, like my mum ten or so years ago, this is new to you, *boner* is an erection synonym. My mum's use of it was brilliantly original. It became her stock text, and sometimes spoken response to good news.

> Me: I will be able to make lunch.
> Mum: Boner!

Boner was a bit of a lexical fad for my mother, but I have retained the notion of an intellectual boner. To this day, I describe all marvellous things as *boner inducing*.

Spunk-water

Certainly an example of the nice prong coated in naughtiness. My home-made perversion of *as dull as ditchwater* is *as amusing as spunk-water*. Spunk-water is not what you think, and though it is not exactly nice, it is fairly innocuous. It is American slang for the stagnant water in holes in tree stumps. *Dull as ditchwater* has become so hackneyed a phrase that it is nearly, well, dull as ditchwater. I think spunk-water is apt to add a little piquancy.

Why don't you come up sometime for Netflix and coffee?

From Mae West's oft misquoted, 'Why don't you come up sometime and see me?' to 'Would you like to come in for a cup of coffee?' to today's 'Netflix and chill?', we have always coined euphemisms for debut sexual threshold crossing. Though I am convinced Mae West would delight in our increased sexual liberation, she might be puzzled that the euphemisms have, if anything, grown thicker. I think the solution might be a euphemism/innuendo melange: 'Would you finish my crossword with me? I need someone to fill in my seven down?' Too much? How about 'Come in for a glass of champagne. I must have company for cork-poppage.' Let's call it a work in progress, shall we?

Depucelated

dee • pyoo • suh • lay • ted adjective verb

Life is full of firsts. Every time we enter a new building or learn a new skill, we are enjoying a *depucelation* of sorts. A *pucelle* in Old French was a 'maiden', and to *de* or 'undo' maidenhood, meant to take one's virginity. Because this word is so rare, should you wish to make a declaration like, 'I am no longer an opera virgin,' but suddenly feel the phrase is malapropos in the setting, you may confidently say, with the very same twinkle, 'I have loved my operatic depucelation.'

Slut-hole

If I told you to shove it in the slut-hole you would think I was being offensive on at least seven different levels. *Slut* and *sluttish* have changed beyond all recognition in their usage. Chaucer talked of sluttish men, meaning that they were unkempt. The slut-*hole* was the receptacle for the slut or clutter in a room. You may, having heard this, suddenly have its innocuous synonym swimming to your frontal lobe. Yes. A bin!

When I'm good, I'm very good, but when I'm bad, I'm better

The aforementioned Mae West delivered this ultimate aphorism on *naughty but nice*. Her 1926 play, *Sex*, scandalised Broadway and saw her briefly incarcerated. However, notoriety turned out to be her friend and she became, arguably, the biggest Hollywood star of the 1930s. When naughtiness has the undergirding of rapier wit and literary brilliance you wind up with something very nice indeed.

How to... speak like a personal trainer verbivore

We might not think of personal trainers and etymology as natural bedfellows, but I am going to make the case against this prejudice. The gym is a panacea for me; mentally and physically. I have often been struck that everything there has a curious name. The odd appellations for the stuff and the exercises in the gym seem to fascinate all who sail in her. The fascination has led to inquiry on the part of personal trainers, which has led, in turn, to some diverting and surprising answers.

Deadlift

ded · lift *noun*

The caveat with the following is lack of proof. What is clear is that this is a compound word using *dead* and *lift*. *Dead* is a contraction of *dead weight*, but here is the etymological rub: was the dead weight in question the dead? Some speculate that this goes back to Ancient Rome and the custom of soldiers *lifting* their slain comrades onto a waiting wagon for a more suitable burial. The losses, the dead weight of the losses and the battle-weary frames of the soldiers tasked with the lifting, all meant technique trumped brute strength when *dead-lifting*. Or so the story goes.

Dumbbells

duhm · belz *noun*

The poet Joseph Addison talked about training with a 'dumb bell' in an article for *The Spectator* written in 1711. It had not yet become a single-word compound noun, leading to the suspicion that primitive dumbbells might well have simply been a *bell* made *dumb* through noisy clapper removal. One can imagine how this might work, providing the bell had a broad enough crown to slip one's fingers through.

Medicine ball

meh · duh · suhn bawl *noun*

Mercifully, we can be a bit more conclusive here. Our beloved Hippocrates, father of medicine, author of the humoral theory, could also be called the father of physiotherapy. In restoring muscles to their pre-injury strength, he realised that, eventually, a little resistance was necessary. He stuffed animal skins to create a weighted ball that could help muscles in the latter stages of their recovery.

Muscle

muh • sl noun

Personal trainers may curdle to learn that *mousy* and *muscly* are, etymologically, the same word. The Latin *musculus* is 'a muscle', but only because the Latin *mus* is 'mouse' and therefore *musculus* is also 'little mouse'. Confused? If you straighten your arm and clench your fist, then contract your arm, you will see the movement of what looks like a small creature under the skin travelling up the inside of the arm. Similarly, if you stand on tiptoes, the same little creature seems to travel up the back of the leg. The Romans thought this moving muscle behaviour was mouse-like!

Gym

jim adjective noun

What is your typical gym attire? Trainers? A tracksuit? Birthday suit? No, your eyes do not deceive you. It does read *birthday suit*. For *gymnos* means 'naked', and that is precisely how those Herculean Ancient Greeks would train. Before I get lost in that thought, I shall plough on with adjacent etymology: *gymnos* also gives us *gymnosperm* or 'naked seed', where the pips and seeds of a plant are not protected by the juicy flesh of various fruit, but are exposed. The most famous example is those of the conifer family.

Pump

puhmp verb

Pump is ubiquitous in gym discourse. Let's pump iron, get our pump on, pump hard and maybe have lunch post-pump? This has real bodybuilder connotations, since the goal for each individual muscle is inflation, like a pumped balloon. And muscles do respond as though freshly pumped. The post-pump selfie is a phenomenon because the muscles have a habit of deflating again in the hours that follow the workout.

AMRAP

Here is a relatively new acronym to me. I am afraid it was an element of the only gym class I have ever exited as fast as I entered. Here comes my excuse. I was at the shank of a week of twelve-hour days. A rather threadbare Tom was first to arrive at what he thought was a gentle resistance class and was told one station was AMRAP. The trainer explained that this can stand for *As Many Reps* (or *Rounds*) *As Possible*. I ran away. In the reps version, you train to failure, when your muscles simply say, 'no more!' In the rounds version, you loop your rounds so that there are no breaks. Sadism!

DOMS

Delayed Onset Muscle Soreness. If you are a gym fanatic, the fanaticism comes, in part, from this feeling. It is hard to describe, but I call it *sexy pain*. It is the pain of having pushed your body without hurting your body. It is the stretching out of muscle fibres in reaction to the exertion you have made them endure. It is one of those invisible phenomena that makes one grow a self-congratulatory inch.

Other PT acronyms

The spitfire acronyms that proceed from a PT's (personal trainer's) larynx can be justified by constraints of talking time. These communication intervals may be as small as the gaps between counting your reps. You are quite likely to hear something like, 'OK! Bit of HIIT (High Intensity Interval Training) to warm up:

start with ten squats, ATG (Ass to Grass). Good! Now high knees, want to hit MHR (Maximum Heart Rate).' After a gruelling warm up you might pump iron, which may result in a new PB. Not a Perfect Bruise but a Personal Best, e.g., highest weight lifted. Imagine the economy of speaking like a PT all the time. This book would be a pamphlet.

The carrot and stick

Here is a euphemism I employ with any trainer I might orbit. *The carrot and the stick* comes from the two ways to galvanise a donkey: a stick for its bottom, a carrot for its eager mouth. It converts, in human terms, into criticism and praise. Because I am too ashamed to tell a trainer that I do not find criticism galvanising, I resort to this phrase. I often say, 'I'm afraid I need rather a large carrot, and a toothpick of a stick.'

How to... allow the culinary to feed our discourse

We are so lucky to live where there is an abundance of food. Stretching through our history, there is also an abundance of food in our language. We cannot resist a culinary coining and they are invariably, pardon the pun, delicious. Etymology, at times, demonstrates how far removed we are from the attitudes of our ancestors, but food etymology does the reverse. Food seldom flies solo. Words concerning food are often accompanied by backdrops and the people who shared the repast.

Breakfast

brek • fuhst noun

Perhaps the simplest word, etymologically speaking, in these pages. *Breakfast* is the 'break' of the 'fast'. I am not talking about a hefty fast, but the natural quotidian fast that is the inadvertent result of a good night's sleep. The first meal taken afterwards will conclude the ingestion interval.

Jentacular

jen • tak • yuh • lah adjective

This word covers all breakfast fare and everything pertaining to it. You might describe yourself as jentacularly abstemious, meaning you have little or nothing for breakfast. You might advocate post-jentacular activities as the optimum time to work or play. You might either stress or pooh-pooh jentacular importance. We owe this rare word to the Latin *jentāculum*, meaning 'breakfast'.

Prandial

pran • dee • uhl adjective

Jentacular is breakfast-specific, whereas *prandial* concerns meals in general. The word comes from the Latin *prandium*, meaning 'meal'. It is a lyrical word that is as successful at softening disagreeable conditions – such as the famous *post-prandial slump* – as it is at conveying the lovelier ones, like *post-prandial dancing*. Incidentally, why do we have a post-prandial slump after lunch but crave a post-prandial scuff of the marble after supper? Food for thought.

Companion

kuhm • pa • nyn noun

Panis is the Latin root meaning 'bread'. The closest child of this root is something that only the upper crust (I could not resist that one) have: the *pantry* or 'bread room'. Of course, those blessed with pantries use them for a great deal more than bread these days. At first glance, *companion* seems to be no companion of our root. However, etymologically speaking, it is a 'person one breaks bread with'. 'Companion', as we use it today, may seem adrift from its root but it is not the only word that metamorphosed, over time, from dining partner to chum ...

Mate

mayt noun

Mate comes from the Old English *meat*, which once meant all food – not just animal flesh. This is why we have terms like *sweetmeats*, which describe the character of that particular *meat* or food. The mangling of *meat* to *mate* came about in exactly the same manner as *companion*. A mate is the prized person with whom you shared your meat.

> To eat and drink without a friend is to devour like the lion and the wolf.
> – Epicurus

Epicurus, the Greek philosopher who advocated the art of discernment concerning food and praised the socialisation promoted by eating, might have coined the words 'mate' and 'companion' himself, given his philosophy. To be *epicurean* was, for a spell, a dirty word. He was dismissed as a hedonist, preoccupied with pleasures of the flesh: lovemaking, eating and drinking. His real preoccupation was with the essential interactions between human beings, of which these activities happed to be excellent examples. 'We should look for someone to eat and drink with before looking for something to eat and drink,' he said. These days, *epicurean* is a word reclaimed to describe the most discriminating palates in the worlds of food and drink. Luciano Pavarotti praised the necessity of having to interrupt the day and devote our attention to eating. Just as the word 'breakfast' acknowledges the natural culinary hiatus the preceding sleep has provided, Pavarotti acknowledged the surcease from the whirligig of life that set mealtimes offer. His were laden with epicurean pleasure. The pleasure of mealtimes is enhanced by the time taken to enjoy them. The *devotion of attention* Pavarotti describes is a form of active meditation. If you are a true epicure, the sensorial overload food provides, plus the serotonin it releases, will flood the brain and may naturally eclipse the anxieties and concerns of the day.

Schmaltz

shmaalts noun

There is not enough Yiddish in this book. At first glance, you may say that this word, that describes the syrupier, saccharine offerings of the arts, is misplaced here. But, like *syrupy* and *saccharine*, *schmaltz's* roots are in the world of food. *Shmaltz*, in Yiddish, means 'melted fat', which is viscous, extremely glossy and devoid of structure. In short, all the things of which artistic schmaltz is accused.

Vittles

vit • tlz noun

Vittles is one of my more selfish inclusions. It is one of my favourite words. It comes from the Old French *vitaille*, meaning 'nourishment'. This transmutation of the word is most popular in the US, as in the Rodgers and Hammerstein culinary song 'A Real Nice Clambake' celebrating the joys of good vittles and company. This is a word that is inherently social. One could happily eat a meal alone, but vittles are for sharing.

Baguette

buh·get noun

I am afraid, and please do not think me puerile, *baguette* takes us straight back to the baculum. If you recall from its entry in *How to describe all your corporeal bits and juices* (*see* page 65), the baculum is the penis bone. It comes from the Greek *baklon*, meaning 'stick' and, of course, the baguette's only synonym in English is the *French stick*. Just think how easily we might have had our veterinarians tending to our cat's broken baguette while we wait in reception nervously chewing a stuffed baculum.

Cafe anthropologist

The lion's share of this book has been written in a cafe. The gentle hum of activity, my private cerebral tap dance while flanked by constant, unwitting inspiration, and the world's most slowly ingested pain au chocolat, are among my local's happy offerings. When I am not here to fill pages with etymological wrestles, I periodically reserve a window seat to watch the world go by. I call this cafe anthropology. It is slightly Orwellian insofar as the observed is unaware of the observer. Their gait, posture, newspaper, sartorial and culinary choices all fascinate me. It is curiously cafe-specific. I am not, I think, nosey by nature. But those lovely, large windows, the galvanising aroma of coffee and the obliviousness of the pedestrian all make me feel like a chief of police observing an interrogation through a two-way mirror.

Polyphagous

po·lih·fah·gus adjective

From the Greek *phagein*, meaning 'to eat' and *poly*, meaning 'many', we humans have as varied a diet as the animal kingdom knows. We are *polyphagous* to the nth degree. We invent jams to

ZWISCHENMAHLZEIT

zwih·shen·maal·zeit *noun*

German, a 'between meal',
to prevent those interminable
stretches between the big three.

go with cheeses for heaven's sake! We even, if put into the jungle, become *entomophagous* or 'insect eating'. We do, however, draw the line at being *coprophagous*, which we leave to rabbits, rodents and dung beetles, the latter being the great connoisseur of *copros* or 'poo'.

Gobbet

goh • buht noun

From the Old French *gobet*, meaning 'mouthful', this word began its life describing mouth or *gob*-sized chunks of food, ideally sized for mastication. The Gaelic word *gob* means 'beak', and we owe both our gobs and our gobbets to it. It is a particularly pertinent word here since these entries are literary gobbets. We live in the age of the literary gobbet with the rise of liberal tweeters. Isn't it interesting, then, that a *tweet* is another beak-centric word?

Marmite

maa • mite noun

I find this word fascinating, especially within the realm of television and radio. The 'you either love it or you hate it' campaign was so successful that the *marmite phenomenon* has superseded the usual brand rules in televised discourse. When appearing on any television or radio programme, one must agree not to mention any brand names. Very occasionally, however, a slogan or name is so well-known that it defies regulation. You could call a divisive character a *marmite person* on television in just the same way you could talk about *hoovering*, as opposed to vacuuming, and the brand attention would be allowed.

Cut the mustard

The etymology of this may have nothing to do with mustard, but it is my favourite phrase concerning food. Many have speculated that this phrase may be a mangling of *cut the muster*, the formal assembly of troops for inspection. If you are a consistently well-turned-out soldier, you may be permitted to cut or miss the muster as a reward. The mangling is divinely nonsensical and has had generations puzzling over what doing something well has to do with as surreal an activity as mustard-cutting.

Curry favour

Favour is one thing that does not curry very well. It is a touch sweet. *Curry* as a verb, meaning 'to groom', is more or less marooned in this single phrase. It comes from the *curry comb*, an item still used for grooming horses. Horses loom large in French allegories, where – given the power of human speech – they even rose to prominence in court and would mock courtiers. The curry comb was a means of being close to the horse, and stroking both his pelt and his ego.

Gingerly

jin • juh • lee adverb

It ought, you might think, to mean *piquantly*. In fact, *gingerly* is almost an antonym for piquantly. It means 'with caution'. The only thing we know for sure about this word's etymology is that it has nothing to do with ginger. It might come from the Old French *gensor*, meaning 'delicate'. It is probable that handling things delicately morphed, gently, into handling things cautiously or *gingerly*.

FUFTB

My paternal grandmother's favourite acronym, heard increasingly when she became a nonagenarian and her appetite grew birdlike. It stands for Full Up and Fit to Bust. Grandma was the only person we – my siblings and I – ever heard say *bust* as opposed to *burst* and was, to us, the only known utterer of this acronym. However, since Grandma is no longer with us, and much of her legacy is in her singular turn of phrase, we all say it when sated, with a twinkle of acknowledgement.

Scoff

skof noun verb

Here is a curious one on many levels. It is a noun and a verb: you may *scoff* your *scoff*. It also has no etymological relationship with its homophone, *scoff*, from the Old Norse *skop*, meaning 'mockery', which has been a part of our language for an additional 400 years. Our culinary *scoff* comes from Georgian slang, which Francis Grose's *Dictionary of the Vulgar Tongue* has taught us was very fertile in the late eighteenth century. Then, scoff was *scaff* and meant to eat rapaciously. Only as the vowel-changed did *scoff* earn its noun stripes.

Happy clams don't clam up

Clamming up would not happen to a happy clam. It is a defence against predators, which is why we have reconstituted this action to describe human reaction to interrogation. My preferred clam-centric phrase is *happy as a clam*. Clams are not always happy, especially at low tide when those pesky winged predators can get at them. But at high tide, oh! – as this nineteenth-century American idiom observed – to be a clam then, is to know true happiness.

How to...
let the music in

If the following sounds outré, please humour me. You see, I think of life in musical terms. You have the gentle libretto of most days. There is the suggestion of an aria here and there, but mostly we deal in recitative. Then life has its truly operatic moments. Regrettably, we are living through a Wagnerian period now. Music provides the perfect metaphor for the undulations, the swells, the ebbs, the horror and the indescribable beauty of life.

Fanfaronade

fan • fah • ruh • nayd noun

I adore this word. It is, etymologically speaking, a 'musical boast', since *fanfarrón* is the Spanish word for 'a boaster'. A *fanfaronade* says, musically, I have something to boast about because here comes so and so or look at such and such. The word itself is so grandiose that it befits the musical peacockery it describes.

Spicy libretto

This is my own coining. The spoken parts of a musical are called the *libretto*. *Life's libretto* implies the constant anticipation of a musical number, which I rather like. Of course, one cannot live from number to number. The finest musicals retain their piquancy in their brilliant librettos. I like the libretto of my life to have a touch of spice.

Blow one's own trumpet

If the fanfaronade is not there to herald an event but a person, the person being heralded is lucky, because their *musical boast* is being done for them. Sometimes, however, we are forced to *blow our own trumpet*. This divides the world into two. The trumpet blowers and the non-trumpet blowers. We are often told that trumpet blowing is an important skill that can result in jobs and advancement. For most of us, however, we would sooner have somebody else perform our fanfaronade. Preferably out of earshot.

Fit as a fiddle

Fit, meaning hale and hearty, has only been in use for the last 200 years. Prior to that, *fit* only meant suitable, as in *fit for a king*. *Fit as a fiddle* originally, therefore, meant suitable as fiddle.

This is, at first glance, rather confusing. In the sixteenth century, a fiddle represented the zenith of both craftsmanship and musicianship. It was, in short, a bastard to make and a bastard to play. It was probably the meagre puddle of excellent fiddle-makers and fiddlers in society that made it such an apt metaphor for suitability.

Face as long as a fiddle

Sticking with fiddles – of the four-stringed variety, naturally – here is a golden oldie that my granny employs. On spying a gloomy countenance, she might quietly observe that 'they have a face as long as a fiddle!' To which, I have found, there is little to say.

He who pays the piper calls the tune

The most egregious of the musical idioms. It is the cry of the tinpot deity: since I have paid for this, I may dictate. To take a little of the odiousness out of the sentiment, it is wrapped in this paper-thin euphemism.

Crescendo / diminuendo

kruh • shen • doh adjective verb
dih • mi • nyoo • en • doh adjective verb

These two words are used to describe musical waxings and wanings. They come from the Latin *crescere*, meaning 'to grow' and *deminuere*, meaning 'to diminish'. Because I think of each day in musical terms, I regard segments of the day as movements that crescendo toward mini social or professional climaxes, and subsequently diminuendo. Do you feel your life is scored, too? It is an inescapable notion for me.

'Music is life itself'

These words, written by Louis Armstrong, are the greatest aphorism concerning music's relationship to life. The two are inextricable. The context makes them even more moving. They were written in 1967 in response to a fan letter from a soldier in Vietnam. In the same letter, he encourages the soldier to 'keep music in your heart' as he talks about the power of melodies to set up camp in the body and live with you always.

Face the music

This idiom, about being bold and doing it anyway, may have had something to do with stage fright. It originated in America in the nineteenth century, and many believe it began as a theatrical idiom. A performer will enter from the wings and, situated between the stage and the audience, is a large orchestra pit, creating a wall of music. Every musical, opera and operetta opens with an overture and the performer(s) in Scene 1 will be in place, behind the curtain, poised for action. They are, quite literally, facing the music and preparing to dazzle, often in spite of fear.

Karaoke

ka • ree • oh • kee *noun*

My favourite Japanese import! *Kara* from karappo, Japanese for 'empty' and *oke* from okesutura 'orchestra'. *Karaoke* technology has existed since 1971 but we owe the name to a musician's strike! The empty orchestra pit prompted radical thinking on the part of the management. The machine was used to accompany the singers, who all seemed to be happy with their pay, if not their new accompaniment.

Macrophone?

ma • kruh • fown noun

Phone is the Greek word for 'voice/sound'. The *xylolophone*, incorporating the Greek *xylon*, meaning 'wood', is a wooden choir or a collection of 'wood voices'. If an orchestra is *euphonious* it is *sweet* sounding, if it is *cacophanous* it is *bad* sounding, since *eu* is 'sweet' and *kakos* is 'bad'. *Phone* has been logically and creatively applied throughout the world of music, with one notable exception: the *microphone*. Vexingly, it means 'small sound', apropos the input sound, which singers will tell you is seldom small. Why is it not concerned with the output sound? The sound for which it was created. A *megaphone* gets its name because what comes out of it is *mega*. What comes out of a microphone is *macro*, or we wouldn't use them. Too late for a rechristen?

March to the beat of one's own drum

Although not advisable in an orchestra, it is sage advice for life. Henry David Thoreau, the nineteenth-century philosopher and essayist, whose greatest study was *Civil Disobedience*, may have coined this. Thoreau's remark, 'If a man does not keep pace with his companions, perhaps it is because he hears a different drummer,' is staggeringly similar. One cannot help but hear the note of admiration in Thoreau's voice here. I, too, am drawn to those that *march to the beat of their own drum.*

How to... successfully close your lexical bin

There are words that are chronically overused. Words that make us curdle. There are words that have a checkered etymological history. We may want to toss them casually into the lexical bin. But they fester there, making a pong, unless we have a ready substitute. Only then can we put the lid on the slut-hole. So, let us have a look at some of vocab's most culpable, and try to relieve them of their duties.

Banter

ban • tuh *noun verb*

Unequivocally the top of my list. Why is my hatred so strong? To begin with, I think the sound of the word is ugly and there is an ugliness to the way it is used. *It's just banter*; the phrase of the early noughties, normally defending everything from the off-colour to the odious. Since this word that used to mean light-hearted, fun discourse is now almost exclusively used euphemistically, can we find a synonym whose meaning is not mangled? I have two candidates: *persiflage* and *badinage*. They both mean blithe, jocular communication and have the added benefit of being delicious to say.

Bingo wings

bin • goh wingz *noun*

This is not really my contribution. My only podcast guest for whom we invented a word bin was Jo Brand. Research had told me there were a few for which she did not care. *Bingo wings* was in first place and is included here because I agree with her. In one tiny idiom, there are many forms of prejudice. It is, quite obviously, fattist. It is misogynistic because it is an aesthetic, female-directed judgment. It is also classist, because bingo halls have remained socioeconomically confined. No alternative required.

Moist

moyst *adjective*

I have no particular gripe with *moist*, but it would be remiss of me not to recognise that it heads most people's rebarbative words list. What is it about 'moist' that is so gut-churning? It conjures all our juices, while also being applicable to dank, disagreeable surroundings, so that it is doubly guilty by association. But something in the word itself, for most people, seems to evoke these things simultaneously Mercifully, one of the loveliest Latin words ever coined is waiting in the wings, longing for her eleven o'clock number (*see* page 25). This word thought its time had come when its child, *humectant*, began to appear on all manner of products that 'retain or promote moisture'. The moisture word at *humectant*'s core is *humectus*, meaning, you guessed it, 'moist'. Why this charming word is confined to Latin lexicon I shall never know. I think it deserves a stonking renaissance.

Man up

Where to begin? I suppose to start with, what are we saying when we state this? A bit like *bingo wings*, one is saying several rather unpleasant things contemporaneously. The first is that men are the stronger sex, or else it would be *woman* up. The second, since it is typically advice imparted to the anxious and fretful, is, be a man and suppress the fret in order to proceed. As we know, fret suppression is the greatest metaphorical backbreaker for men. 'Man up' also denotes a kind of muscling through, the 'up' suggesting a sort of matter over mind phenomenon. I know there will be some readers who think, 'Oh come on! It is merely semantics.' I disagree with this notion totally. Since children are listeners and imitators, some of the first lessons they learn are in the unconscious biases found in everyday discourse. Root out the most odious and we will change the way people think. And alternatives? I think anything from our chapter on *How to be brave* (*see* page 99).

Pus

puhs noun
Pus is never far behind *moist* on hated word lists. It is, even

Threadbare

thred • behr *adjective*

A word to describe extreme fatigue, lack of inspiration, and the bloom being off one's rose.

etymologically, repugnant, poor thing. It is a relative of the Latin *puter*, meaning 'rotten' which gives us other words devoid of charm like *putrid*. Also, like 'moist', it contains that 's' at the end which seems to squelch and squirt and seep out of the word as an 's' is apt to do. 'Pus' is deserving of our sympathy, as it has the clear disadvantage of not being a nice thing. This we can never change but there is, I am happy to say, an attractive synonym for it. *Sanies*. Directly translated, this means 'a thin greenish foul-smelling discharge from a wound, ulcer, etc, containing pus and blood.' This is Latin but, unlike *humectus*, it is not confined to Latin. So, our job in this case is merely one of popularisation.

Grow a pair

As with 'man up', I am contemptuous of the fact that the male strength bias is so strong that we do not even have to complete the sentence. We know we are not talking mammaries. Apart from the obvious problems with this phrase, too numerous to list, anatomically this is a very vulnerable area, as is well documented. There are parts of the female anatomy which are far more robust, elastic, resilient. But again, let's not fall into the slut-hole of matter over mind. Matter never wins, anyway.

Flap

flap noun

Again, I have no flap problems, or even problems with *flap*, per se. But 'flap' sends shockwaves through tympanic membranes everywhere. Why? Could it be the corporeal conjurings? The near-onomatopoeic nature of the word? A suggestion of mild panic? Though I am not in the curdle club when it comes to 'flap', I would suggest a table *leaf* would work as an extremely attractive and successful synonym.

No offence

I am prepared to bow to popular opinion on this one. I find myself invariably tickled by the mini-warning, 'no offence, but ...' giving just enough time to brace oneself for the ensuing offensive remark. I am also tickled by the notion that saying 'no offence' will successfully remove the sting of the offensiveness of the rest of the sentence. However, I must share the aversion on some level since *no offence* is a phrase that I would never utter myself. No offence.

Belch

belch *verb*

Belch is my *moist*. It is a burp that contains a squelch, which I cannot help but attribute to the presence of a little sick. Most burp words, including *burp, gurk* and *eructation* sound almost arid, irrespective of their etymology. *Belch*, conversely, sounds wet. Given the preponderance of synonyms, may we toss it headlong into the lexical bin?

Vibes

vibez *noun*

It's odd. I have nothing against 'vibrations'. Far from it. But I have taken a dislike to *vibes* of late. Occasionally a word is so widely applicable that its time of being in vogue sees it used to the point of absolute exhaustion: 'What takeaway would you like?' 'I feel Italian vibes!'; 'Nice outfit: Hepburn vibes!'; 'I just get bad vibes.' It has become as frustratingly indistinct a word as *energy*. When a word is that vague, it must be binned. 'Vibrations', conversely, retains a clarity. A good vibration is a palpable feeling that somebody or something is emitting and you are receiving. The word has kept all its sexy physicality.

OBMUTESCENCE

ohb·myoo·teh·sns *noun*

When one is rendered mute
by situation or circumstance,
'forgive my momentary
obmutescence.'

A Final Word

One of the real delights of this book is that I have been able to impart my personal lexical favourites. Through mapping the words and phrases that have tickled, moved and inspired me to the extent that they are indelibly seared on my mental retina, you may find a few leap from these pages and brand your own frontal lobe. In that way, dearest stranger, you and I will share something forever. I think in words, as opposed to images, so the libretto of the lives of others is what seems to capture my imagination most. *Accent*, etymologically speaking means 'the song of a region', and it delights me that through our regional songs, coupled with our personal lyrics, one can regard all of humanity as one vast choir.

If you have reached this point, you have ingested and possibly digested the whole book. Now we are bound forever by words. Language is inherently reductive. That is why a preverbal baby or an animal will disarm you with their gaze. They do not listen to your words but instead read your soul. They are less concerned with what you present but read who you *are*. But as adults we belong to civilisations. We require words to procure and convey very necessary things. Therefore, to my mind, lexical greed is the one exemption from the sin of gluttony. In a world of bulletins, let us find nuance. If you become practised in colour, detail and nuance, you will eventually find the perfect word is always ... on the tip of your tongue.

Thanks

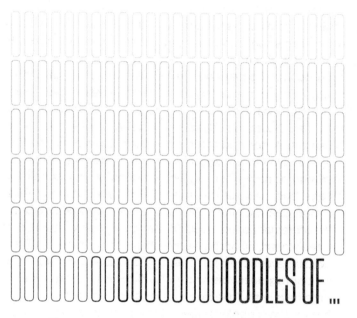

oo·dles *noun*

Origin unknown – lots of. Chiefly for things we crave: oodles of fun, oodles of rose and violet creams and oodles and oodles of love.

I consider myself enormously fortunate to be bolstered and buoyed by so many. In terms of language, my greatest influence was always my father. He loves the very taste of words. I defy anybody in his orbit not to experience referred pleasure at his palpable delight in language. My mother gave me a window into another tongue altogether. We have a weekly French lesson in which she will play piquantly with idioms from across the channel with *l'entrain éternel*. Other family members and friends have nourished my spirit. My brother, Jack, and sister, Miranda, have been hugely hortatory throughout this process. They have a faith in me that extends beyond my own at times. Thanks to my aunt, another English teacher, who makes toothsome submissions to my 'Word of the Day' posts, including, incidentally, 'toothsome'. I must also thank her daughter, my cousin, Niamh, with whom I get to play in the lexical sandbox of gender fluidity. All my chums have a rub-off kind of vim, but I could not have done this without the ears of Julie and James Lawes, James, Charley, Mitch, Becks and Guy. I love you all dearly. The aforementioned 'buoying' was chiefly required because, at the start of all of this, authorship was entirely new to me. I would never have been brave enough to attempt it without the contagiously derring-do brilliance of my agent and, these days, friend, George. Equally benevolent in guiding me through the scribbler's labyrinth were my mentors at Quarto: dear Katie, Ramona, Phoebe and the terrific team. Thank you, too, to dear Susie Dent, my kind, munificent big sister of logophilia. Finally, I must thank you, the reader. Many of you have fuelled my penman's pipedream by requesting a book in the comments beneath my 'Word of the Day' posts. A seed was planted and, almost without my noticing, grew. Your digital exhortations have been invaluable to me.

Oodles of love, Tom x

Index

Also available
by Tom Read Wilson...

Every Word Tells a Story